Scott Rankin is the Creative Director of Big hART. His projects have been included in the Sydney, Melbourne, Adelaide, Perth, Brisbane, Ten Days on the Island and Edinburgh festivals, and toured Dublin, London, Nederlands, Sweden, Iceland, South Africa, New Zealand and Germany. Scott's work includes *Namatjira* (national tour), *Ngapartji Ngapartji* (national tour), *Nyuntu Ngali* (Windmill and STC) and *Box the Pony* (Leah Purcell). Scott is renowned for creating works in varied genres—such as the award-winning outdoor public housing work *Stickybricks* (Sydney Festival), the floating video installation piece *Junk Theory* (Sydney Festival), the international hit comedy *Certified Male* with Glynn Nicholas, large-scale film and radio installation project *Drive In Holiday*, and experimental works like *Beasty Girl*. Scott has won three Green Room Awards for Best Direction and Most Innovative Production, and a Sydney Theatre Award for Best New Work for *Namatjira*. Big hART receives awards from many different fields for its theatre, film and community cultural development work, including a World Health Organisation Award, an AFI Award, eight Coalition of Australian Heads of Government Awards, a Deadly Award and recently the Myer Performing Arts Group Award.

Trevor Jamieson in Ngapartji Ngapartji, *2009* Big hART *and Belvoir production at Belvoir St Theatre in Sydney. (Photo: Heidrun Löhr)*

Namatjira
written for the Namatjira Family (Aranda)

Ngapartji Ngapartji
written for Trevor Jamieson (Pitjantjatjara)

Two plays by **Scott Rankin**

CURRENCY PRESS
SYDNEY

CURRENCY PLAYS

First published in 2012
by Currency Press Pty Ltd,
Gadigal Land, Suite 310, 46-56 Kippax Street, Surry Hills NSW 2010
enquiries@currency.com.au
www.currency.com.au

Namatjira first published by Currency Press in 2011.
Introduction copyright © Sophia Marinos, Alex Kelly and Scott Rankin, 2012.
Namatjira © Scott Rankin, 2010, 2012; *Ngapartji Ngapartji* © Scott Rankin, 2006, 2007, 2012.

COPYING FOR EDUCATIONAL PURPOSES

The Australian *Copyright Act 1968* (Act) allows a maximum of one chapter or 10% of this book, whichever is the greater, to be copied by any educational institution for its educational purposes provided that that educational institution (or the body that administers it) has given a remuneration notice to Copyright Agency Limited (CAL) under the Act. For details of the CAL licence for educational institutions contact CAL, Level 15/233 Castlereagh Street, Sydney, NSW, 2000; tel: within Australia 1800 066 844 toll free; outside Australia +61 2 9394 7600; fax: +61 2 9394 7601; email: info@copyright.com.au

COPYING FOR OTHER PURPOSES

Except as permitted under the Act, for example a fair dealing for the purposes of study, research, criticism or review, no part of this book may be reproduced, stored in a retrieval system, or transmitted in any form or by any means without prior written permission. All enquiries should be made to the publisher at the address above.

Any performance or public reading of *Namatjira or Ngapartji Ngapartji* is forbidden unless a licence has been received from the author or the author's agent. The purchase of this book in no way gives the purchaser the right to perform the plays in public, whether by means of a staged production or a reading. All applications for public performance should be addressed to Big *h*ART, ph: 61 3 6423 4577, andrew@bighart.org.

NATIONAL LIBRARY OF AUSTRALIA CIP DATA

Author: Rankin, Scott, 1959–
Title: Namatjira & ngapartji ngapartji / Scott Rankin.
ISBN: 9780868199221 (pbk.)
Subjects: Australian drama–21st century.
Other Authors/Contributors:
　　　　Rankin, Scott, 1959– Namatjira.
　　　　Rankin, Scott, 1959– Ngapartji ngapartji.
Dewey Number: A822.4

Typeset by Dean Nottle for Currency Press.
Cover design by Emma Vine for Currency Press.
Cover images: (front) Trevor Jamieson (Pitjantjatjara man) in *Ngapartji Ngapartji*, 2009 Big hART and Belvoir production. (Photo: Heidrun Löhr); and (back) Trevor Jamieson in *Namatjira*, 2010 Big hART and Belvoir production. (Photo: Brett Boardman)

Contents

Introduction
  Sophia Marinos, Alex Kelly and Scott Rankin   vii

NAMATJIRA   1
  Act One   7
  Act Two   28

NGAPARTJI NGAPARTJI   47

Currency Press acknowledges the Traditional Owners of the Country on which we live and work. We pay our respects to all Aboriginal and Torres Strait Islander Elders, past and present.

Derik Lynch (Yankunytjatjara man) in Namatjira, *2010* Big hART *and Belvoir production at Belvoir St Theatre in Sydney. (Photo: Brett Boardman)*

Introduction

These two seminal works for theatre were written by Scott Rankin, with social innovation company Big hART, through a unique creative process spanning 2005 to 2011. These uniquely Australian stories have graced the stages of the country's major festivals and most prestigious venues, as well as being performed outdoors in dry riverbeds in some of the country's most isolated and remote communities.

Utilising Big hART's unique creative process, they have grown from, and been developed with, the communities where these stories originate. *Namatjira* was created with the extended families descended from the acclaimed artist Albert Namatjira, who come from Western Aranda country, west of Alice Springs. It was through their generosity, along with that of Gayle Quarmby (Rex Battarbee's daughter), that this piece resonates with authenticity and heart. Similarly, *Ngapartji Ngapartji* was created thanks to the gift of the Jamieson family's story—of diaspora in the face of the Cold War British Nuclear testing on their homelands—and the generosity of the Pitjantjatjara community in sharing many aspects of their language, culture and wisdom.

Both these theatre works are bursting with stories that go right to the heart of the intersection between indigenous and non-indigenous experience in this country. Both are interwoven with the depth and breadth of common human experience. They are stories of family, friendship, land, myth, life and death, with all the peaks and troughs that touch us all. They celebrate life, and its complexity, diversity and adversity. They are contextualised within the social, political and historical framework of their times, locally, nationally and internationally. This may be part of the reason for their box office popularity—they resonate universally, yet at the same time capture unique moments in Australian history and experience.

Namatjira and *Ngapartji Ngapartji* are part of a long line of critically acclaimed plays written by Scott Rankin, a number of which have been invitations from, or collaborations with, indigenous people and communities. These works include *Box the Pony* for Leah Purcell, and

Riverland for Ian W Abdulla and Wesley Enoch. Scott and Trevor Jamieson have maintained a rich, collaborative relationship, working together for over ten years on many productions including *Namatjira, Ngapartji Ngapartji, Nyuntu Ngali, Career Highlights of the Mamu, Knot @ Home* and others. Now, with *Namatjira*, Scott is also working with the remarkable Derik Lynch on new works.

Big *h*ART has been producing long-term intercultural projects such as *Namatjira* and *Ngapartji Ngapartji* for twenty years. Big *h*ART is a not-for-profit, social change, arts company made up of artists, producers, arts workers, community builders, field workers, and researchers. The company strives to create exquisitely finished art at the same time as working with the country's most marginalised communities and individuals, providing opportunities for individual change, community change and social policy change at a national level.

Big *h*ART tries to experiment with this process of making art, over a minimum of a three-year period, utilising varied artforms such as theatre, film, television, painting, photography, dance, new media and radio.

Remarkably, over this time, Big *h*ART has emerged as Australia's highest producing and most critically acclaimed arts and social change company. From 2004 to 2011 Big *h*ART presented twenty works, to high acclaim, in festivals in Australia and overseas. Since its inception in 1992, Big *h*ART's programs have assisted over seven thousand people experiencing severe disadvantage in forty-two communities across Australia, assisting many of them to make sustained changes in their lives.

It is against this backdrop that these two projects emerged, these two plays were created, and these two scripts are being published. *Ngapartji Ngapartji* is the product of work with Pitjantjantjara communities, and *Namatjira* with Western Aranda communities.

Ngapartji Ngapartji

The *Ngapartji Ngapartji* project headquarters were based on Arrernte country in Mparntwe (Alice Springs, Central Australia) between 2004 and 2009. The *Ngapartji Ngapartji* theatre production was one part of a much broader project which included ninti.ngapartji.org, an online Pitjantjatjara language site; a long-term arts language-based community development program throughout the Central Desert; an ABC documentary, 'Nothing Rhymes with Ngapartji'; a language policy campaign; and the acclaimed theatre production.

'*Ngapartji ngapartji*' translates roughly as 'I give you something, you give me something', a concept of reciprocity which governs relationships in Pitjantjatjara society and culture. This concept of reciprocity underpinned the entire project—reflected in the working practice on the ground, where skills in language and arts practice were equally valued and shared across cultures and generations; and in turn, the website and theatre shows offer an opportunity to participate in a rare and intimate experience of language and culture.

At a policy level, the project sought to highlight the dire status of indigenous languages and help generate a national and international groundswell of support for the maintenance and preservation of these languages. Behind these over-arching goals is the fact that Australia has witnessed the largest and most rapid loss of languages of anywhere in the world, over the last century. According to the 2005 National Indigenous Languages Survey, the situation of Australia's indigenous languages is 'very grave and requires urgent action', and Australia has been identified as the place with the most rapid and widespread loss of indigenous languages anywhere in the world over the last one hundred years:

> Of an original number of over 250 known Australian indigenous languages, only about 145 indigenous languages are still spoken and the vast majority of these, about 110, are in the severely and critically endangered categories.

In response to this the *Ngapartji Ngapartji* project, together with a group of indigenous language professionals devoted to helping languages to thrive, was successful in facilitating the Federal Government to announce a National Indigenous Languages Policy in 2009. There is still a way to go, but this is one of the many legacies of this project in co-operation with others.

The work of the *Ngapartji Ngaparjti* project over six years in Alice Springs and the Central Desert also paved the way for the *Namatjira* project to be conceived and developed.

Namatjira

At its inception, the *Namatjira* project was a small idea to tell a big story. Elton Wirri, a kinship grandson to Albert Namatjira, had been touring the country with the *Ngapartji Ngapartji* production. When introducing Elton to audiences at the conclusion of the performances, it became clear that they wanted to know more about Albert Namatjira, and so, gradually this project developed, working with the families and communities descended from the renowned painter.

> My name is Lenie Namatjira, I'm the granddaughter of Albert Namatjira... and I would like to say something about my grandfather. I'm happy that you mob can tell this story... people from all over the nation can see, what we're doing, this lovely painting.
>
> Lenie Namatjira
Granddaughter of Albert Namatjira

Namatjira is also a multilayered project. It is a creative community development process; a touring new Australian theatre work; a touring contemporary watercolour exhibition; a strategy to assist the Namatjira family to be able to take trips to paint 'on country' in important places; teaching watercolour painting to younger generations; a film and documentary process; working with, and recording the Choir in Hermannsburg; and a contribution to social policy discussion around the vital role of Indigenous Art Centres and remote indigenous communities.

At the core of the project is a partnership with Ngurratjuta 'Many Hands' Art Centre in Alice Springs. Ngurratjuta supports contemporary Central Desert watercolour artists, many of whom are grandchildren and descendants of Albert Namatjira and artists from the original 'Hermannsburg School'. The national *Namatjira* tours and accompanying exhibitions of vibrant watercolours aim to leverage greater income and exposure for the contemporary school of Central Desert watercolour painters.

Growing from this partnership with Ngurratjuta, the *Namatjira* project has made it a focus to support Indigenous Art Centres more broadly. Art Centres are owned and governed by Aboriginal people, and are a vital part of community life. Often the only source of externally generated income in remote communities, they are hubs for innovation, creativity, cultural expression, non-welfare-based income, local leadership, health and wellbeing.

As part of the ongoing *Namatjira* project, Big *h*ART continues to engage Federal Ministers and policymakers in discussions to highlight the unique opportunity Indigenous Art Centres present to help build sustainable communities.

It is with true thanks that we acknowledge how much these two projects and the stories contained within them continue to teach us, about creativity and resilience.

Sophia Marinos, Alex Kelly and Scott Rankin

Sophia Marinos is the Creative Producer for the *Namatjira* project.
Alex Kelly is the Creative Producer for the *Ngapartji Ngapartji* project.

For more detail on the *Namatjira* and *Ngapartji Ngapartji* projects, visit these websites:

www.namatjira.bighart.org.
www.ngapartji.org
www.bighart.org

Trevor Jamieson (Pitjantjatjara man) (left) and Derik Lynch (Yankunytjatjara man) in Namatjira, *2010 Big hART and Belvoir production at Belvoir St Theatre in Sydney. (Photo: Brett Boardman)*

Namatjira
written for the Namatjira Family (Aranda)

Namatjira was first co-produced by Big *h*ART and Belvoir at Belvoir St Theatre, Sydney, on 25 September 2010, with the following cast:

PERFORMER	Trevor Jamieson (Pitjantjatjara man)
PERFORMER	Derik Lynch (Yankunytjatjara man)
MUSICIAN	Genevieve Lacey
PORTRAIT ARTIST	Robert Hannaford
SECOND MUSICIAN	Nicole Forsyth
SECOND PORTRAIT ARTIST	Evert Ploeg

Grandchildren and descendents of Albert Namatjira performing as artists on rotation throughout the Belvoir season:

Kevin Namatjira
Elton Wirri
Gloria Pannka
Ivy Pareroultja
Hilary Wirri
Lenie Namatjira
Betty Wheeler
Mostyn Kentaltja

Co-directors, Scott Rankin and Wayne Blair
Set Designer, Genevieve Dugard
Costume Designer, Tess Schofield
Composer and Music Director, Genevieve Lacey
Sound Designer, Jim Atkins
Lighting Designer, Nigel Levings
Creative Producer, Sophia Marinos
Assistant Lighting Designer, Christopher Page
Stage Manager, Luke McGettigan
Assistant Stage Manager, Jessica Smithett
Sound Operator, Nick Shipway
Associate Producers, Cecily Hardy and Clare Atkins
Community Producers, Shannon Huber, Sia Cox
Social Policy, Pru Gell

Cultural and Family Consultants: Lenie Namatjira, Kevin Namatjira, Betty Wheeler, Mostyn Kentaltja, Gloria Pannka, Ivy Pareroultja, Kevin Wirri, Joseph Rontji, Rahel Engwaneke, Judith Ingkamala, Gayle Quarmby.

Big hART's *Namatjira* project is a long-term, multi-layered arts and community development project, with a touring performance piece and a grass roots project working with Aranda people in Alice Springs and Hermannsburg. For more about the project and about Big hART visit www.namatjira.bighart.org

MAIN CHARACTERS

JONATHAN NAMATJIRA (Western Aranda name: NAMATJIRRITJA), Albert's father

EMELIE (Luritja name: LJUKUTA), Albert's mother

ALBERT NAMATJIRA (Western Aranda name: ELEA)

REGINALD 'REX' BATTARBEE (later named UNTJWAARA by Western Aranda men), whitefella landscape artist

WILMOT, old blackfella living in the Warrnambool forest

PASTOR, at Lutheran Hermannsburg Mission, speaks a blend of German and English

RUBINA (Western Aranda name: ILKALITA), Albert's wife

OTHER CHARACTERS

ARMY SERGEANT, Fifty-Eighth Battalion
ARMY MEDIC, at Bullecourt, France
BAKERY EMPLOYEE, in the inner city
MISSION MEN, at Hermannsburg
AUSSIE BLOKE 1 & 2, tourists
KID, at mission
MELBOURNE SOCIETY WOMAN
CHARLES MCCUBBIN, prominent artist
LADY HUNTINGFIELD, wife of the Governor of Victoria
MR T.H. GILL, a pompous gallery owner
CUZ 1, 2, 3 & 4, mission humbuggers
WHITEFELLA 1 & 2, in Alice Springs
OLD ARANDA MAN, elder
GOVERNMENT MEMBER, in Parliament
OPPOSITION MEMBER, in Parliament
GOVERNMENT MAN, bureaucrat
MAURICE, one of Albert and Rubina's sons
MAISIE, one of Albert and Rubina's daughters
SYDNEY SOCIALITE
QUEEN ELIZABETH II, Queen of England
NEWSPAPER REPORTERS
MAGISTRATE, Mr Dodds, a Senior Magistrate

SETTING

The action of the play takes place in various Australian locations during the lifetime of Albert Namatjira (1902–1959).

The stage features several large sculptural shapes, made of wood, creating a variety of landscapes and locations.

To one side is a portrait artist with easel, and a chair in which his model sits from time to time.

Two other artists (from the Namatjira family) are drawing a large black-and-white landscape in chalk across the back of the stage.

HYMNS

The following hymns appear in the text.

'Fierce Raged the Tempest' (p.9)
Words: Godfrey Thring; Music: John Dykes (1862). Arranged by Genevieve Lacey. Translated into Western Aranda by TGHS (1964).

'Follow On' (pp.16 & 23)
Composed by Rev. W.O. Cushing (1878). Arranged by Genevieve Lacey. Translated into Western Aranda by David Roennfeldt.

'Kumbaya' (p.19)
Traditional. Arranged by Genevieve Lacey.

'Stille Nacht!' ('Silent Night') (p.28)
Composed by Franz Xaver Gruber (c.1818). Arranged by Genevieve Lacey. Translated into German by Carla Verwer.

'Abide With Me' (p.45)
Composed by William Henry Monk (1861). Arranged by Genevieve Lacey.

ACT ONE

SCENE ONE: NAMES

As the audience enters, TREVOR *is being painted by a portrait painter. He is seated on a chair next to the artist's canvas. The house lights remain up.*

TREVOR: *Wertai.* Trevor, Trevor Jamieson... See how I managed to get my name in the first line? Clever.
> *'Wertai'* is Arendt for hello. So now I'd like you to try it, say *'Wertai'*...
> *The audience responds.*

Nice one. Again? *Wertai...*
> *The audience responds.*

My mob are Pitjantjatjara—and for hello we say *'Wai palya'*. Albert Namatjira was Arendt, or rather, now they'd say—Western Arendt, which can be spelt Arendt, or Arrente, or Aranda. Those crazy Aranda mob, not like us sensible Pitjantjatjara [*spelling it out*] P.I.T.J.A.N.T.J.A.N... J.A.R.A... I think.

Let me introduce you to a few people. [*Indicating*] This here is... Kevin, Kevin Namatjira—Albert's grandson. Here... Elton Wirri—great grandson, kin way. And Derik Lynch—related also. And here, Genevieve Lacey [*the musician*] and Robert Hannaford [*the portrait artist*]—they're not Aranda. Guessed that, did you?

Tonight the Namatjira family have invited us to share their grandfather's story. So I'll be playing—or 'channelling', if you will—characters, in no particular order. Well, they'll be in order, otherwise the show wouldn't make sense, would it? And you'd all be sitting there like this... [*looking like a pondering theatre type*] thinking, 'Mmm, indigenous theatre, so intriguing, such rich cultural idioms'. So tonight I'll be playing Albert Namatjira—which is lucky, given the title of the show, and all the posters and everything. Make more sense than say... Brett Whiteley or someone.

But before we get started, let you in on a secret. 'Albert'—not actually a traditional Aboriginal name. Who'd have guessed, eh? Albert was named after a Pommie king, by a German missionary, in the Lutheran tradition, during Federation. See, blackfellas stealing your culture again? Truth is, Albert was not even his name. His name was not even Namatjira—that was supposed to be his father's name. Except it wasn't. Because his father's name was… Namatjirritja.

He pauses while the painter continues painting him.

Funny thing, eh, how in Australia when people are naming their kids, they don't pick any of our beautiful Aboriginal names, like… Membaatha, or Markinti, or Namatjirrtja. We choose Italian names, sure—Anna Maria—and Greek names—Alexandros—even exotic British names like, umm, Nigel. But why not those beautiful names from the heart of our country—the oldest of all names? I wonder why…?

Chances are there'll be some couples here tonight, recently pregnant. Imagine the pillow talk after the show when they get home: 'Markinti is a nice name.' 'But, do you think we have to ask permission?' 'Do we need a… "Welcome to Name"?' 'Is there such a thing as an indigenous-naming-protocol consultant we can hire?'

Anyway, sorry, where was I? Albert's father—Namatjirrtja—came in from the bush, early last century, to the foot of a mountain we call *Ndaria*, to something new and mysterious, called a Lutherische mission. A German one. And he was a bit worried, see…

NAMATJIRRITJA: [*in Aranda language*] Iwana nana? [*English*] What dis 'Lutherische'?

TREVOR: He didn't know, poor fella, Hermannsburg Mission. German one.

NAMATJIRRITJA: [*Aranda*] Iwana nana? [*English*] What dis 'German'?

TREVOR: Came in at the 'turn of the century'.

NAMATJIRRITJA: [*Aranda*] Iwana nana? [*English*] Who dis 'century'?

TREVOR: He was an important man, for the Namatjirritja…

> The Flying Ant… flying,
> Down from Mount Sonder,
> Along the shimmering Finke River, out over Ormiston.
> He knew these places deeply, before,
> Before the mission,

Before they changed his name to Jonathan,
He taught his son these things.
And so too, one day Albert will need to tell his sons, of his father's country...
And they too, their sons... and so on.

[*Indicating*] And see there?
That Namatjirritja... hovering, looking down,
Sees something, there, on the horizon,
Another kind of ant, mechanical one, trail of dust, see...?
A Model T ant... and it's coming, from the east.

DERIK *brings* TREVOR *a shirt, which he puts on at the portrait chair.*

DERIK *and* TREVOR *sing the hymn 'Fierce Raged the Tempest'.*

DERIK: [*sung, in Aranda*]
Ilkankula yurrangkaka,
Kurtungurl' etna trerraka;
Unta kanh' ankw-intarlanga,
Kunpinya.

DERIK & TREVOR:
'Kamerrai', etna ilkaka
'Paarrp', Ingkaartai,
tangkalhelai!'
Wurinyanh' unta turnaka:
'Rrukerrai!'

Ilkankula yurrangkaka,
Kurtungurl' etna trerraka;
Unta kanh' ankw-intarlanga,
Kunpinya.

SCENE TWO: WARRNAMBOOL, VIC.

TREVOR: Over east, at the turn of the century...
In a small Victorian town—Warrnambool—
A baby is born,
Reginald Battarbee, or 'Rex' to his mum and dad.
Scrawny, white, big-nosed country boy,
Grows up good way, in the bush.

And up behind his house there, in Selby forest,
In a tin humpy,
An old man of the *Kuurn Kopan Noot*,
Named... 'Wilmot'... lives alone.
Not many left now, and
Young Rex, often stares, shy.

One day he waves.
Old Wilmot, watching out across the plain,
Waves back at this scrawny knock-kneed kid.
And then... Rex kicks a stone, running home... but curious, see.

Later, grown-up, after school, Rex'd visit old Wilmot...
Sit and look and listen... laugh,
Yellow teeth, tobacco-fingered, different words,
By the fire, singing... hints of another country.
Who could he be, this old man?

YOUNG REX: Hey, Wilmot. How come they say you're the last of your people?

SCENE THREE: ARE WE THERE YET?

TREVOR: Same time, out there,
Albert's father, Namatjirritja—*Pilthara* skin—
Married Ljukuta—*Mpitjana* skin.
And together they walked about naked,
As they always had done, and,
Through them, also, a baby was born who we knew as Albert.
They named him Elea. Carpet Snake Dreaming.

It was the time of the long drought,
And it took its toll,
They walked many miles searching for water, food,
For their little one.

NAMATJIRRITJA: [*Aranda*] *Pitjai! Elea. Ljukuta, Pitjai! Pitjai!*

TREVOR: They'd heard of a place where strange people gave you food, you could *ilkultja* [*eat*] all you want... and *ntjuma* [*drink*] all you need... at Ntaria. But little Elea—toddler now—was slowing them down/

DERIK: [*as Elea, Aranda*] *Narna kala etinya-erraka?*
TREVOR: [*as Elea*] Are we there yet?
DERIK: [*as Elea, Aranda*] *Narna kala etinya-erraka?*
TREVOR: [*as Elea*] Are we there yet?
DERIK: [*as Elea, Aranda*] *Narna kala etinya-erraka?*
TREVOR: [*as Elea*] Are we there yet?

SCENE FOUR: REX JOINS UP

A boxing bell clangs.

TREVOR: In Warrnambool,
 With white bread and bush rough and tumble, time passes,
 And young Rex grows up and out of forests and forgets.
 But Old Wilmot doesn't change,
 He shrinks a bit, coughs a little more, watches Rex take off.
 And now, with school finished,
 With friendships, and news of war, rumours of adventure,
 Rex joins up: 'Too easy, mate'.
ARMY SERGEANT: Company dismissed! Fall out!
TREVOR: And then months of training later,
 He's striding now, down that road to his house,
 Uniform, crisp 'n' collar tight,
 Gut full of butterflies,
 Turns on spit 'n' polish boot, marches home,
 To show his mum,
 So she'll be proud,
 Before the trucks come,
 Before mates come,
 Before they take off to the city,
 To docks, to ships… to where?
 God only knows…

SCENE FIVE: COMING TO HERMANNSBURG

DERIK: [*as Elea, Aranda*] *Narna kala etinya-erraka?*
TREVOR: [*as Elea*] Are we there yet?
DERIK: [*as Elea, Aranda*] *Narna kala etinya-erraka?*
TREVOR: [*as Elea*] Are we there yet?

NAMATJIRRITJA: [*like a white dad*] Shut it! Not another word! Bloody sick've it. When I was your age, I had to bloody walk across the Simpson bloody Desert, barefoot, 'luxury'. But you try telling that to kids today.

TREVOR: Or words to that effect. Except not so much in English, obviously, never even heard English when they arrived at that mission.

NAMATJIRRITJA *sneaks into the mission.*

PASTOR: [*German*] Guten Morgen.

NAMATJIRRITJA *gets a shock.*

NAMATJIRRITJA: Ahhhh!

TREVOR: They arrived at Ntaria, Hermannsburg Mission. Elea, exhausted, hungry, the little family defeated by the drought.

PASTOR: Guten Morgen. Ohhh, look at the little kleinkind here.

He pats Elea's head.

Ahhh, Essen und trinken… ja? Kom.

TREVOR: Most children, born out there, were dying, starvation. The mission had flour for damper, and sugar.

NAMATJIRRITJA: *Pitjai, Elea, pitjai, Ljukuta!*

NAMATJIRRITJA *likes what he sees and gestures to the others to come.*

TREVOR: And tea.

NAMATJIRRITJA: *Elea, Ljukuta, pitjai, pitjai!*

TREVOR: Traditional way—where there's food, you stay, see. So Namatjirritja, Ljukuta stayed. And from then on they'd come and go from the bush, for business.

He moves like a flying ant.

SCENE SIX: LANDING ON THE BEACHES

The flying ant movement has become the movement of the ocean.

REX *is on a ship. It is pitching. We hear the sea, the wind, the pounding of the bow into the swell, the creak of the hull. A ship's bell sounds.*

TREVOR: December 30, 1916. Fifty-Eighth Battalion. Somewhere out in the English Channel, before dawn, Rex is feeling queasy, scared, alone.

ARMY SERGEANT: Easy, Private, easy.
REX: Sergeant?
ARMY SERGEANT: What's your name, son?
REX: Reginald, sir. Battarbee. Rex Battarbee. Private 2616.
ARMY SERGEANT: Well, Private, take it easy, son, breathe. Soon as you hit the beach, you'll find your feet, you'll be right.
TREVOR: Coast of France looms out of the dawn. He smells the salt and sweat and country-boy puke. Rex, all white knuckles and butterflies, pressed forward, to gunwale, to ropes, to landing boat, beach... to some unknown enemy, German were they, or...?

The percussive sound of boots.

SCENE SEVEN: HERMANNSBURG WEDDING

A wedding cereony at which the family are given new names by the Lutheran PASTOR. NAMATJIRRITJA *will be known as* JONATHAN, LJUKUTA *as* EMELIE, *and* ELEA *as* ALBERT.

TREVOR: At Hermannsburg...
PASTOR: So, we are gathered here today to, uh... [*Seeing* NAMATJIRRITJA] Sorry... und... was war ihr name... Namatijira, ja?
NAMATJIRRITJA: Namatjirritja.
PASTOR: Nam-at-jiiirji?
NAMATJIRRITJA: Namatjirritja.
PASTOR: Nam-at-jiiir? Nama-vateva. I taufe you, Jonathan, in the namen of the Herrn Jesus Christus. Ljukuta, I taufe you Emelie, in the namen of the Herrn Jesus Christus... und the little kleinkind, here, Elea, I taufe, mmm, let's see... Albert, after your king... ja? So. We are gathered here today... I now pronounce you man und Frau. You may kuss your braut, ja? Kuss.

He shows them how by kissing himself.

As the little infant ALBERT *is taken by the hand, he is not happy.*

ALBERT: Maaam! Maaamai!
TREVOR: Times are hard at Hermannsburg. The Lutherans are doing their best. But there's almost no water... food is scarce. No money, government won't help. New babies, born, die in their mother's arms.

He shows this.

PASTOR: Herr Jonathan, don't you want jung Albert to be in einem sicheren ort... safe, in the dormitory/
TREVOR: The Pastor thinks little Albert will be able to eat and drink and learn. And his parents'll still be close by, outside, round their fire. They can still see each other anytime. And Jonathan and Emelie want this for Albert.
ALBERT: Maaam! *Maaamai!*
JONATHAN: Go on, inside, now! *Pmara-urna Alpai! Lhai!*
ALBERT: Maaam! *Maaamai!*

He stops as he eats the food he is given.

Mmmm... yum...
TREVOR: So now the Namatjira family have a new friend, their boy is safe, they give him food off their own table... and teach him the fascinating language of the white man.
PASTOR: Say after me, 'Guten Morgen, Pastor'.
ALBERT: Guten Morgen, Pastor.
PASTOR: Repeat after me, say 'eins'.
ALBERT: Eyns.
PASTOR: Not eyns, 'eins'.
ALBERT: Eins.
PASTOR: Gut. 'Zwei'?
ALBERT: Zwei.
PASTOR: Gut. Say 'drei'.
ALBERT: Drei.
PASTOR: Okay. 'Vier'. Okay, okay einverstanden, in ordnung... Eins, zwei, drei, vier...

SCENE EIGHT: BULLECOURT, FRANCE

The sound of a World War One battle overwhelms.

REX: One... two... three... four...

An explosion. More canon fire and explosions.

TREVOR: In France, in the trenches, Rex too is learning to count...

A single canon shot rings out loud, then silence.

REX *is counting and listening for the shell to explode.*

REX: One… two… three…
Another explosion.
Black.

TREVOR: In the muddy fields of Bullecourt,
    Ten thousand dead and tangled limbs,
    Rex, buried, bleeding, shell-shocked, gassed, feels nothing,
    Face, chest, shoulder shattered,
    Medics… weave,
    Bullets scream, stretchers, screamers,
    Glance at Rex, silent, life leaking…

ARMY MEDIC: Hold on, mate. We'll be back. [*Aside*] Done for, I reckon.

TREVOR: Under fire, they take those who might just make it…
    Rex, left for dead, dying…
    In the long waiting hours,
    Rex, drifts in and out,
    Three days and nights pass,
    Mass grave dug, bodies dragged,
    Till/

ARMY MEDIC: This one, alive I think. Is he?

A shell explodes close by.

TREVOR: Days later, Rex wakes to a stench of death and nurses.

A song from the Hermannsburg Choir.

SCENE NINE: AT THE MISSION

The PASTOR *is seated at the portrait chair.*

PASTOR: *Pitjai!* Kom! *Pitjai! Ilkutjika, ilkutjika,* essen, eat, *nama, nama,* sit and be.

TREVOR: The Pastor, much loved,
    Baking, serving, feeding
    Three hundred each day shelter from the drought.
    Bush mob in for food, fix 'em up, send 'em out.
    Preached his much-loved gospel, in German.
    Every day.

PASTOR: *Pepa… Pitjai…*

TREVOR: Devotions.

PASTOR: Freizeit…
TREVOR: Refresher Bible study, every day the Aranda would sit and listen… They understood he was a spiritual teacher. Sometimes, though, it seemed a bit mixed up. The missionaries'd say…
PASTOR: The Holy Spirit will come and 'leben in euren Herzen'—'live in your hearts'.

They show us how the Aranda people are terrified.

DERIK: Hey! Ahhh! *Irintja!*
TREVOR: They'd used the word *'irintja'* as in 'scary ghost'.
PASTOR: And because God loves you, the 'scary ghost' will come and live in your hearts, isn't that wonderful?!
DERIK: *Yakai! Irintja! Yakai! Irintja!*
TREVOR: They needed the word *'etetha'*—meaning 'a living person's spirit'—still a bit scary. Or they'd say…
PASTOR: Dumust follow Jesus.
TREVOR: To explain 'follow' the Pastor used the word for 'tracking' as in 'tracking to kill'. Made the songs a bit funny. So, instead of singing *'Follow, follow, I will follow Jesus'*, they sang *'Tracking to kill, tracking to kill, I will spear Jesus'*. But Aranda mob were generous, they helped… the Pastor changed it to a word which meant 'walk in front of you'.
　'Walk in front of you,
　Walk in front of you,
　Because I completely trust you, Jesus,
　To walk behind me and not kill me,
　Even though you are carrying a very sharp spear…'
It didn't scan quite as well, but you know…

DERIK brings TREVOR a blue shirt, which he puts on.

TREVOR and DERIK sing the hymn 'Follow On'.

TREVOR & DERIK: [*sung, in Aranda*]
　Atha Jesu-nha kuta lurnamanga,
　Kutatha, kutatha,
　Atha lurnama.
　Atha Jesu-nha kuta lurnamanga,
　Era yinganha kutatha,
　Rretjingamanga.

SCENE TEN: REX IN HOSPITAL

REX: Nurse! Nurse!
TREVOR: Field hospital. Rex, stunted, stricken, hallucinates.
REX: Nurse! Get my things, we're heading out!
TREVOR: Weeks turn to months. Operation follows operation. Bullets lodged were pulled.
REX: Nurse! Nurse? You know what this place needs? Something pretty to look at. Maybe I should paint your picture.

He is slapped.

What!?
TREVOR: Months later, Rex, crippled, shipped from England...
REX: So, nurse, if you're ever in Warrnambool, Australia, and you're looking for a crippled husband with two gammy arms, who can't work, and has no money and no prospects, you'll know where to find me, okay—

He is slapped again.

TREVOR: Three years, convalescing. One hand a shrivelled claw. Elbow shattered. Out of hospital, like many returned soldiers, can't work. Takes it hard. Legs are good, though. Walks, out through the bush, every day, up to where old Wilmot still lives. Striding like some skinny-legged waterbird. Family say nothing. Rex sits looking out over that plain, trying to make sense of it all.

SCENE ELEVEN: MISSION

TREVOR *is seated on a rock.*

TREVOR: Albert is growing up now,
　　And life in the mission goes on as usual.
　　Many Aranda stayed out bush, under stars,
　　By the fire, on the clean sand,
　　But Aranda way was a hard way.

　Out there,
　　When the mob walked waterhole to waterhole,
　　Old people'd slow everyone down,
　　Endanger the family in the heat,

> So one morning, kindly, before leaving camp,
> Your children'd bring you extra food,
> They'd touch your hand,
> And you'd know your time had come…
> And as they left, you'd stay, in the cool shade,
> With food for a few days… to die.

Now if only the baby boomers would take that advice.

The Pastor stood up for those old people. Was he doing the right thing to speak up? I don't know. It's easy for us to criticise, sitting at our favourite, inner-city footpath café, of a Saturday morning, sipping a decaf soy latte, reading Nicolas Rothwell in a weekend newspaper… Should the Pastor have spoken up for these old people? Was he weakening the culture?

PASTOR: Was ist richtig? Was ist falsch? I don't know.

TREVOR: The Pastor welcomed these old people to the mission. Was he wrong? What would we do? I'm sure, when we see a homeless old blackfella, shuffling past our tastefully renovated, inner-city terrace, we welcome him in to break bread—a nice gluten-free, sourdough roll from the Bourke Street Bakery perhaps.

An EMPLOYEE *from a trendy inner-city bakery café steps forward.*

BAKERY EMPLOYEE: Hello. Come in, come in. We had to like queue for twenty minutes. But, you know, have some, please, it's fine. Where did you say are you from? Aranda mob? Right, right. You don't happen to know any interesting indigenous baby names, do you?

SCENE TWELVE: REX LEARNS TO PAINT

REX *moves like a waterbird.*

TREVOR: Two thousand miles away, in that Warrnambool forest, old Wilmot watching Rex.

WILMOT: Reginald! Reginald… is that you?!

TREVOR: Young Rex… with his gammy arms, in the grasslands below, sitting, painting in private, trying his hand at watercolours…

WILMOT: You back now? You walk funny. What're you painting there? Heron? Flies down here this time of year. Sees the whole country, that one. You walk like him.

WILMOT *tries to be still while* REX *paints him.*

TREVOR: Rex, quiet, paints. His sister—bohemian, parlour painter, Heidelberg School—showed him watercolours.

WILMOT: Wherever the rains come, he knows this country. Seen him walk?

TREVOR: Rex listens… paints. Watercolour is for womenfolk. He wants to paint in oils, but the turpentine stings his damaged skin. So now he's crippled, useless, unemployed, and paints like a girl. It's going very well. But out here, with old Wilmot, he's happy enough.

WILMOT: So, your wing is clipped… Watch that bird. He knows the belly of the country… fix you up, that one.

REX: I wish he'd stay still, buggered me painting now.

TREVOR: Rex might paint like a weakling, but he loves to walk… with his paints… loves the bush. Maybe he could head out there, paint that country nobody sees. Bring it into people's houses, make a quid. So he starts saving his pennies. Buy a car, head out. Like a frugal little waterbird following the rains, in a second-hand Model T Ford.

TREVOR *puts on a vest.*

TREVOR *and* DERIK *sing the hymn 'Kumbaya'.*

TREVOR & DERIK: [*sung, in Aranda*]
Ingkaarta pitjai, nuk-urna!
Ingkaarta pitjai, nuk-urna!
Ingkaarta pitjai, nuk-urna!
Ingkaarta pitja!

Relha irtnima, Ingkaarta!
Relha irtnima, Ingkaarta!
Relha irtnima, Ingkaarta!
Ingkaarta pitja!

SCENE THIRTEEN: TIME FOR BUSINESS

A Sunday school hymn is sung.

ALBERT *approaches* JONATHAN, *his father.*

JONATHAN: Elea, Elea! *Pitjai! Ntjaantja kurna-ntama Ntwaarra Ilai!* [*'Elea! You stink, get away from me! What is that?'*]

TREVOR: Jonathan sniffs his son. Scent of soap and water… of bread and wine and Sunday school.
ALBERT: Safe soap, father.
TREVOR: Albert, scrubbed to within an inch of his life. Mahogany skin shining in the sun like good Christian skin.
JONATHAN: That's not richtig, that way. But hey, I want some of that safe soap for mich-also. Now, geht spielen! [*Seeing the* PASTOR] *Wertai*, Pastor, entschuldigung. Pastor, can I have a word?
PASTOR: Was ist los?
JONATHAN: Mein junge Elea.
PASTOR: Albert, yes?
JONATHAN: Ja. Albert. He's heranwachsend—growing up now. Be hairy soon. Ein stolzer moment. Proud of him. He needs to go bush with the men for Gesetz—law… kulture. Proper way.
PASTOR: Mitbringen to die Kirche. Church. Sonntag, er, Sunday school. He comes with us now, yes?
JONATHAN: Ja, Pastor, Sonntag school.
PASTOR: That old way is vorbei.
JONATHAN: Eh?
PASTOR: Finished, here at the mission. Essen und trinken.

He shows him food and drink.

Gut, ja?
JONATHAN: Ahh. Eat and drink—*Marna ilkuntjamia pa ntjuntjamia*—We won't go then, Pastor. We'll stay here… Danke, Pastor. Vielen dank.
PASTOR: Gott segne dich, mein Sohn. Bless you.
JONATHAN: [*directly to the audience*] Albert'll be a man soon.
    Elea has to come with me sometimes,
    And sometimes he has to stay.
    I love Gott. Pastor has songs, Aranda have songs.
    They have ancestors, we have ancestors…
    Sacred things, Aranda also…
Pastor is just a bit bossy about his Gott, that's all, but he doesn't know… [*Calling*] Elea! Albert, get your things, we go!
ALBERT: But, you said I'm supposed to stay, Father.
JONATHAN: Don't worry, your mother'll tell him we've gone walkabout.
ALBERT: What this walkabout?

JONATHAN: Don't know, but whitefella think we do it all the time… Could come in handy in years to come!

SCENE FOURTEEN: FALLING IN LOVE

TREVOR: So Albert, teenager now, taken… out bush, away months… become a man, proper way, with his uncles… But he's a typical adolescent. [*He shows us.*] Got his hoody, iPod, skinny jeans with his arse hanging out.
JONATHAN: Hey, time to go now, son.
ALBERT: Busy here.
JONATHAN: Time to go.
ALBERT: Do I have to?

Music: Barry White's 'I Can't Get Enough of Your Love, Babe' plays under.

JONATHAN: [*directly to the audience*] Kids today. Oldest culture in the world, given him everything, Carpet Snake Dreaming, boomerang, those little stick things you bang together. Can't tell 'em, eh.
TREVOR: Trouble is Albert is a bit distracted. Seen a hottie—young Ilkalita—Luritja woman…

He watches ILKALITA *from behind a bush. She is shy for him.*

Problem… out of his range. Champagne taste, beer budget.
ILKALITA: Albert, Albert, where for art thou, Albert?
TREVOR: So anyway, they fall in love.

ALBERT *and* ILKALITA *make eyes at each other.*

TREVOR *and* DERIK *sing a duet, 'I Can't Get Enough of Your Love, Babe', in English, with Aranda backing vocals, as a dance number.*

So basically, they elope and ride off into a beautiful… watercolour… sunset…

They climb on a Harley and ride away.

SCENE FIFTEEN: RETURNING TO THE MISSION

PASTOR: Es gibt immer sehr viele/
TREVOR: /The pastor often found himself arguing with government in his crazy half German/

PASTOR: /Es gibt immer sehr viele lebensmittel food here... how you say?... Sammlung, jagen, übernehmen, was benötigt wird... umm, hunting, ja?/
TREVOR: There's always been plenty of food in the bush—gathering, hunting, taking what's needed. But the cattle now eat the grass down/
PASTOR: They leave nothing for ahm der känguruh/
TREVOR: He says, the kangaroo leave, then there's nothing to hunt. And the cattle trample the bush tomato, and the berries. And too much grazing... means no grass seed for flour to make bread.
PASTOR: There used to be plenty of warser... but you have to look after the warserholes/ but der Aborigine, teil der ureinwohner Australiens, have a strong, strong ahm stinken ahm duft ahm scent.
TREVOR: They're proud of that scent... but it scares the bullock away. So the cattlemen drive the blackfellas away from the waterhole, in favour of their other 'animals', their cattle. And out there is where Albert and Rubina are living—beyond the reach of the Pastor, beyond his father and uncles—those two young lovers. Eloped, for three years, in that beautiful tough country... walking waterhole to waterhole. Two babies born... no babysitter, no Huggies, no help. And so, sensibly, they say...
DERIK: Fuck dat.
TREVOR: So Albert and Rubina decide to try their luck back to the mission.
EMELIE: Albert, my boyyyyy, what you run off like that for?!
TREVOR: Actually, Derik, it was a bit more blackfella way.

> DERIK *gives a tiny nod and lip point.*

'I'm overwhelmingly happy to have you back, Albert, everything is forgiven, I don't know why you took so long.'
EMELIE: But do that again and I'll slap you! Now, how many kids you got...? Only two? What's wrong with you!?
DERIK: See, Trevor, that's blackfella way!
TREVOR: So Albert and Rubina decide to stay at the mission, and the Pastor is pleased. Got good jobs waiting. Satisfying ones, like... making brooms. So that good. Albert quickly moved up in the world... to making shoes. Excellent. And finally... stockman. Day off Sunday for recreation—basically making babies and singing in the choir.

> TREVOR *and* DERIK *sing another verse of 'Follow On'.*

TREVOR & DERIK: [*sung, in Aranda*]
    Atha Jesu-nha kuta lurnamanga,
    Kutatha, kutatha,
    Atha lurnama.
    Atha Jesu-nha kuta lurnamanga,
    Era yinganha kutatha,
    Rretjingamanga.

TREVOR: So there was Albert, between two worlds. Name changed. Not a man, not a boy. Following his heart western way, wrong-way marriage. Speaking Aranda, German, bit of English. He's an evangelist, choir, bushman. Growing family, poor, no house, nothing. *My*, hasn't the world changed?

    A Model T Ford arrives.

Then one day into the mission comes this angry mechanical ant. And from its belly climbs this strange little man... and he walks funny, like a bird.

    MISSION MEN *gather, aroused, whispering.*

MAN: *Aiyua untjwarra era pitjika/*
MAN: *Alte reiher mann ist gekommen/*
MAN: *Aiyua untjwarra era pitjika/*
MAN: Old Heron Man has come.

    REX *steps from the car, moving like a heron.*

SCENE SIXTEEN: REX ARRIVES AT NTARIA

TREVOR *and* DERIK *and the* MEN *are looking at Rex's watercolours. They can't believe what they see. They look behind, then wave their hands in front of them, talking and pointing to each other.*

MAN: *Yakai! Nhanha aria! Yakai! Nhanha aria! Yakai! Nhanha aria!*
TREVOR: Biiigg commotion... because...
    Right before their eyes, this man
    Does the strangest thing,
    Puts little magic squares,
    Against the mission wall, like windows,
    Places from miles away, frozen in time.
    Places of ceremony.

Special places,
Caught, perfectly real, like…

A movement hinting at the flying ant…

… if you were small enough you could climb right in…

… and waterbird.

… and… this other thing we've never seen this way, so bright it almost hurts our eyes… like the sky.

MAN: Hey, Iwana nana… what's this here?
REX: Well, son… that's… that's what we call 'blue'.
MAN: Hey?
REX: Blue.
MAN: Blue?
REX: Nearly, now one more time… Blue.
MAN: Blue… Alkira?
REX: Yeah, sky blue.
MAN: Mara.
PASTOR: [*introducing*] Ahhh, Rex, dis ist Albert. Albert, this is Herr Battarbee.
REX: Call me Rex.
ALBERT: Rex?
REX: Rex.
ALBERT: Rex. Oh… like a dog.
REX: Yeah, Rex.
ALBERT: Marra… how do you make magic windows?
REX: Well, Albert, it's called 'water-colour' and/
PASTOR: Farbige wasser. Coloured water.
ALBERT: Coloured water? Ohhh, kwatja-lela paint mpaarai!
REX: Yeah, whatever ya reckon. Use a brush and/
ALBERT: Oh, like broom. I'll make you a brush and you can teach me to paint?
REX: Well, it's not easy, Albert, but we can give it a go.
ALBERT: How much, for these?
REX: To sell, you mean? Ten guineas, maybe twenty.
ALBERT: Oh, twenty guineas.
TREVOR: Albert wanted some of this blue magic. Not for the art, for money. To stop making stupid brooms. To feed the kids, get Rubina off his back.

PASTOR: Rex, Albert is also kuhjunge. Cowboy, stockman, und a kamel reiter.

REX: Kamel? Cameleer, eh? I've been looking for one of those. Model T keeps getting bogged.

ALBERT: I can take you. Places no-one has ever seen, by camel, and you can teach me to paint and you can teach me to speak English, proper way.

REX: Cameleer, eh, well that's ruddy terrific.

TREVOR: [*to the audience*] So, how do you like my whitefella acting? It's not easy for us, you lot all sound the same: 'Cameleer, eh?' You all sound like the Leyland Brothers to us. I could slap on a little whiteface, maybe that'd help. But, politics, politics…

He returns to the portrait chair.

Anyway… So, Albert takes Rex out bush to paint. He bakes damper, hunts, cooks for them and, in exchange, Albert watches this strange new magic way of seeing. Not the meaning of country… but the way country looks. Not the totems, but the place… the mirror of it. A different way, a new way, a clever way, a strange way, an easy way, a hard way, a money way. And he watches this strange, little, half-crippled waterbird… and he quite likes him.

ALBERT: So, Rex, how do you do it, your way, can you show me?

TREVOR: Rex gives him crayons and cardboard.

REX: Well now, you look and you paint what you see, see?

TREVOR: But Albert didn't see… and he's worried.

ALBERT: But, Rex, I can't just paint what I see.

REX: I know, everybody thinks that at first… Now, see how the light falls on those rocks there… Or the sun on that rivergum, the edge is bright and silvery white—that's the white of your paper—then you lay the colour in washes… Time and practice, you'll be painting alright.

ALBERT: But, Rex, I'm not allowed to look at everything. You see, some places are not for men, and some the women's, some places are not mine.

REX: Riiiight… Well, now you're scaring me.

TREVOR: Albert is worried that if he paints someone else's country, he might reveal things without permission—someone's totem. Like out at Simpson's Gap, there are dangerous things there, lizard men climb the sheer rocks, everywhere he'll have to leave things out.

Same for whitefellas. You have this sacred totem I've heard of—a donkey, I think? A man and his donkey, who once—in one of your dreamtimes—defied death for a few days, in a big war some place, and now every year they become more sacred.

Grandkids, when they hear that story, when they hear that spooky horn, weep tears for the grandfathers and great-grandfathers. Ancestors to them, we understand this.

And no-one should make fun of that donkey, because in that donkey totem is the essence of the white people... I think. And so every year in a sacred place called Canberra, people gather at dawn, and a strange, slow, marching dance is done. And, I think, although it's sacred and I have to be careful how I talk about it, and I have to ask permission, I think your dreaming goes like this...

Once upon a time a brave donkey helped a man to rescue other dying men for a few days, in a futile war, against some Turkish people who were shooting them, without really knowing why, because they weren't the real enemy, I think, because a few years before that a couple of European, inbred royal families had upset each other, by not apologising for something that never really happened... or something...

Anyway, that donkey and the sacred Simpsons are very important. And we shouldn't talk about them except on special occasions each year, or when visiting the big bronze donkey statue, or when visiting a gap near Alice Springs, which is sacred to us—but has been renamed Simpson's Gap—where the tourists stop in buses.

AUSSIE BLOKE 1: Nice, eh? Named after that donkey bloke, wasn't it?

AUSSIE BLOKE 2: Yeah. Nice the way the sun catches on the red cliffs, and the silver gum. Geez, it's hot though. What do you reckon? Back on the bus, eh?

TREVOR: They don't mean any harm, looking and seeing nothing. Lizard men, [*showing us*] climbing... That Albert can't paint, they're sacred—Aranda way—like that donkey. Only much, much older. So Albert knows he will have to paint differently to his new friend. Yes, he'll learn to paint for the white people with the money. And yes, he will hide things—he is learning to walk both ways.

ALBERT: Hey, Rex. Can you show me how to paint, with the brush?

REX: Well now, Albert, baby steps, baby steps... These are very expensive colours. They come all the way from Europe. A Mr Windsor and Mr

Newton make them… and interestingly, they also sponsor this show tonight, and in white culture, this is what we call 'product placement', and they are 'the finest paints in all the world'. So first, try some crayons, on these cardboard boxes—'the finest boxes in all the world'.

ALBERT: Danke, Rex, thank you. One day maybe you can help me sell my paintings, and I'll support my family this way.

REX: Alright, Albert, well how's about we let these good people go to interval, then?

ALBERT: *Iwana nana?* Who this 'interval'?

END ACT ONE

ACT TWO

SCENE ONE: CHRISTMAS

During interval TREVOR *is being painted by the portrait painter.*

DERIK *enters with a candle, in procession with the musician who is playing a recorder.*

DERIK *sits on a rock, as a Namatjira child.*

DERIK *and* TREVOR *sing 'Silent Night'.*

DERIK & TREVOR: [*sung, in German*]
    Stille Nacht! Heil'ge Nacht!
    Alles schlaft; einsam wacht,
    Holder Knab' im lockingen Haar,
    Schlafe in himmlischer Ruh!

ALBERT: Rubina… Rubina… Other kids have a tree. Supposed to have snow, proper Christmas—German one. Any biscuits tucked away?

KID: Biscuits, yeaaahhh! Biscuits!

TREVOR: Albert drags an old Mulga branch home, sticks it in the dirt outside the hut.

KID: Yeaaahhh! Old Mulga branch!

TREVOR: No tinsel, hang some baked bean cans on there.

KID: Yeaaahhh! Baked bean, yeaaahhh!

TREVOR: So, there they are… ninth baby just born. Poor as a bush mouse.

KID: Bush mouse, yeah!… Bush mouse?

TREVOR: Humpy, seven kids all crammed in, dirt floor, spotless though. But two little ones finished now… scurvy. Kids all hungry most of the time. Albert, a nobody. How do you look your family in the eye? In the hope of earning money, Albert's keeps trying his hand at… landscape… looking at Rex's picture of Mount Giles hanging above the Pastor's desk.

    ALBERT *is painting.*

ALBERT: Needs something more, this, but…

TREVOR: Albert has earned a penny making a broom.

ALBERT: Here, kangaroo on there, hoppin' fast way… copy that one.

    ALBERT *keeps painting while looking closely at his penny.*

PASTOR: Albert, been out bush you have, I see, captured the kangaroo perfectly.

ALBERT: Well, sort of… special blackfella way of seeing… kind of.

PASTOR: Vat do you call it this one?

ALBERT: Um, he called 'hopping kangaroo', I think… proper traditional one.

PASTOR: To Adelaide, ja. I'll take for you to sell, six pictures, if you finish, ja?

ALBERT: Thank you, Mr Pastor.

    ALBERT, *on his knees, prays. The mission bell rings.*

TREVOR: Five shillings each. The Pastor sells nothing. So he buys two pictures himself… to encourage Albert, gives him the money.

    ALBERT *holds the money.* RUBINA *takes it gently out of his hand.*

RUBINA: Thank you.

TREVOR: That's what we call 'Welfare Quarantine', blackfella style. Good fella, that Pastor.

SCENE TWO: STOCKMAN

DERIK: But Australia wasn't built on the missionaries' back. No sir-ee, built on the sheep's back.

    TREVOR *and* DERIK *sing 'Where the White Faced Cattle Roam' by Lee Kernaghan.*

Yee-ha!

TREVOR: [*becoming a white cattleman*] That's what I'm talking about.
    Australia was built on the back of the bullock,
    The cattle, the stock.
    And who were the best stockmen?
    Them blackfellas.

DERIK: Yee-ha!

TREVOR: Tame ones at least.
    Brilliant they are,
    Nothin' they can't bloody do.

> Not enough whitefellas like me, see,
> And gee they can work,
> On horseback, bloody terrific to watch, natural.

He cracks a whip above DERIK.

> Can't get enough of 'em,
> Feed 'em up
> They're happy,
> Good for 'em.

He cracks the whip again.

> Round 'em up,
> Pair a trousers,
> Hat, a horse, bully beef,
> Same as pay to 'em.

He cracks the whip again.

> And the women,
> Pretty little things, aren't they?
> Bit lonely out there, like a loyal pet really,
> Plenty of cute little blue-eyed bastards, runnin' barefoot, eh…
> mum's the word.

He cracks the whip again.

> TREVOR *and* DERIK *sing a reprise of 'Where the White Faced Cattle Roam'.*

It's alright but, mission brings 'em in. Take me hat off to 'em, but geez they can be interfering pricks. Always onto government, whingeing. We built this country on the back of the sheep, the bullock, and the Black—not careful they'll be givin' 'em the vote soon.

DERIK: [*sarcastic*] Yee-ha!

SCENE THREE: FIRST MELBOURNE EXHIBITION

TREVOR: So there's Albert… good stockman. Big man. Strong. Nice wrangler butt. Bootscootin' good. But now he's friends with Rex and they see this new thing. This new way. Albert, with his eight kids, a way out of poverty. He wants it bad and Rex can see it too.

REX: Albert, I have to head back to Melbourne.

ALBERT: *Iwana nana*, who dis 'Melbourne'?

REX: Don't give me that 'who dis Melbourne' bullshit, we did that in Scene One. Big city place, lot of people. They like to buy art.

ALBERT: Mmm… What for?

REX: Well, for their drab suburban walls, to make 'em feel posh or something, I could maybe take some of your pictures, if you want, just to see.

ALBERT: Okay… but why don't they paint their own?

REX: Albert, you crack me up, you crazy old philosopher.

TREVOR: So Rex takes five of Albert's paintings, and hangs them, as a curiosity, in his own exhibition. With a donation box for anyone who wants to help. People are just so fascinated…

The family artists make their way on stage.

KEVIN NAMATJIRA, *one of the family artists, helps* TREVOR *put on a red shirt.*

MELBOURNE SOCIETY WOMAN: Just gorgeous… And to think their primitive minds can see the world as we do. Of course, one can't be expected to hang a picture by an unknown Black in our living room but, sixpence could be handy, buy themselves some soap, perhaps. Did you read McCubbin's comments in the papers?

MCCUBBIN: Remarkable how this Aborigine has grasped so readily the European conception of art. His painting of Mount Hermannsburg is outstanding in its realism, light, and form. Together, the Aborigine's knowledge of tone and colour value is extraordinary.

SCENE FOUR: PAINTING TRIP WITH REX

TREVOR: 'Down the beautiful, sandy Finke River,
  Where the sheer red sandstone cliffs, scored by wind and rain, shoot up out of the white riverbed,
  Where the ghost and the rivergum glow like white giants, in sun harsh against the distant mauve horizon,
  Where the spinifex shimmers in pale green tufts across the silence…'

Sorry, I'm sounding all Banjo Paterson…

A year later, out painting together… Albert cooks stew and tea and damper, tends camels, and of an evening, in the silence of the bush, for months on end, these two men sit quietly, and they talk art and culture and eat and learn from each other. Over the crackle of burning Mulga, Albert learns English and teaches Rex Aranda...

ALBERT: Hey, Rex, say with me, *'werta'*.
REX: Umm, *werta*?
TREVOR: Perhaps it's hard for us to glimpse the strangeness of this. Rex, a digger, sitting alone, far from anything, in a riverbed with... a 'native' considered part of the 'flora and fauna', discussing art.
ALBERT: [*teaching him*] Say it with me, Rex... *Alkira*—sky blue.
REX: *Alkira*.
ALBERT: *Marra*. Now *arna*—orange dirt.
REX: *Arrrna*?
ALBERT: Not *arrrna—arna*.
REX: *Arna. Marra.*
ALBERT: *Parta*, red, like the sandstone hills in your painting here. Colour, is perfect. [*Sung*] *'Ntulya marr inthurra nhanha.'* [*Chanted on one note*] 'Painting very good this.'
TREVOR: And Rex tries to say something like...
REX: *Marrama unta mpuarama!* Umm, you're doing well there, Albert... *Erinha* paint... um, *inthurra nthaka, parnitjika*.

SCENE FIVE: MELBOURNE AND LADY H

TREVOR: And again, after months painting, Rex returns to Melbourne. This time he takes more of Albert's paintings than his own. 'Society' has heard the name Namatjira now. There's a buzz at the opening. Everyone is there—the Governor and his wife... the divine Lady Huntingfield.
LADY H: When I was in Alice Springs recently I met the extraordinary Albert Namatjira and watched him work. And I said to him... Albert, now that you are going to be famous, what shall we call you?
ALBERT: Albert, marm.
LADY H: And I said to him... No, of course, but I mean, you can't just sign your pictures Albert... What's your surname, your family name?
ALBERT: Didn't know I needed another... um... [*signing*] Albert... Nam...at...jira.
LADY H: Oh, lovely... What does that name mean?
ALBERT: Nothing.

NAMATJIRA 33

LADY H: Oh, how interesting. It's your family name, is it?
ALBERT: No. It's a made-up name, for my father.
LADY H: Oh, like a nickname? What was his name then?
ALBERT: *Namatjirritja*. 'Flying Ant'.
LADY H: [*looking around, horrified*] Where?! Where?!
ALBERT: My name is Elea, or Taranga, but I'm Albert because... I don't know why. He's called Jonathan Namatjira, expect that isn't it, so I'll use the name that isn't his for the name that isn't mine/
LADY H: And you know, I thought to myself... Isn't the Australian Aborigine interesting? And on that note I declare this exhibition open. I thank you.

>LADY H *bows and waves.*

TREVOR: Yes, thank you, Derik... what pretty calves she has. All of his paintings sold in three days, for six guineas. More money than Albert had ever known. For the first time he was getting out of this grinding poverty. And from then on he signed his pictures Albert Namatjira. And he took his family bush for a year, painting, without Rex. All his favourite places, special places. And on that trip, while they were out there, Rubina gave birth to their tenth child—Maurice. And this man here...

>*He goes over to* KEVIN NAMATJIRA, *one of the family artists.*

Kevin Namatjira, is Maurice's son. And Kevin is one of the family who has asked us to tell this story tonight.

SCENE SIX: PAINTING TRIP WITH FAMILY

TREVOR *is about to throw a spear.*

TREVOR: A year, living bush way, hunting, finding good bush tucker...

>*He throws the spear, killing an animal.*

So good, Albert lost four stone... and made thirty paintings. For Rex though, it's still hard to convince anyone to exhibit him, to help Albert and the mission, but he manages to line up one gallery—T.H. Gill's, with the paintings at twenty-five guineas each...
MR GILL: Now, Rex, dear boy, with regards to the catalogue, we need something for the cover. A picture perhaps of this Albert fellow...

naked... with a spear maybe... on one leg... by a fire. On top of Ayers Rock... cuddling a koala... do you think?
REX: Well, I'm not so sure I/
MR GILL: You said he paints in the bush.
REX: He does, but/
MR GILL: Living in the traditionally.
REX: Yes but/
MR GILL: Eating bush tucker.
REX: Yes, but he also speaks three languages. He's an educated man.
MR GILL: That is a pity.
TREVOR: The exhibition sells well. Again, more money than Albert's ever known.
CUZ 1: [*gesturing*] Hey, Uncle, money please?
ALBERT: [*handing some over*] There you go.

>ALBERT'S RELATIVES *suddenly come from different directions, all asking.*

CUZ 2: Hey, Uncle?
CUZ 3: Me too, Uncle?
CUZ 4: Uncle, over here?

>ALBERT *makes his escape.*

TREVOR: Albert builds Rubina a nice new home by the Finke River. Good house, stone, one... two room, spotless, modern.

>ALBERT *proudly opens the door for* RUBINA.

ALBERT: Light globe here, look. I'll just start the generator.
RUBINA: Who this 'generator'?
ALBERT: [*to the audience*] See where I get it from?

>*He starts the generator.*
>Family all there, feeling proud.
>ALBERT *and the family are preparing to sleep.*

KIDS: 'Night Ewald/ 'Night Maurice/ 'Night Maisie/ 'Night Enoch/ 'Night...

>*The sound of the generator gets noisier as they try to sleep.* ALBERT *can't sleep. He gets up suddenly.*

RUBINA: Ehhh, this light too noisy, eh, I'm going down the river.
KIDS: Me too/ Me too/ Yeah, too noisy, eh.

SCENE SEVEN: HE SUPPORTS SIX HUNDRED PEOPLE

CUZ 1: [*pointing*] Albert there, see?
CUZ 2: Which way?
CUZ 1: There, see?
TREVOR: The community has never known money like this. Albert is starting to have to support the whole extended family. Six hundred people now.
CUZ 1: Hey, Uncle!
CUZ 2: He's not your uncle, he's my uncle.
CUZ 1: He is so my uncle.

>ALBERT *picks up a truckload of people.*

Can I have a lift, Uncle?
ALBERT: Git on up.
CUZ 2: [*to* TREVOR] Hey, Uncle, you're sounding a little 'James Brown' there.
ALBERT: Come on then.
CUZ 1: Where we going?
ALBERT: *Alapring*. Town.
CUZ 2: Party up… Got any money, Unc?

>ALBERT *gives money.*

CUZ 1: Me too, Uncle, sorrow business.

>*He gives more money.*

TREVOR: So there they are. Alice Springs. Party in the riverbed—outdoor motel. Newspapers take photos of them.

>*A camera flash.*

WHITEFELLA 1: Can't handle their liquor. It's sad really.
WHITEFELLA 2: Haven't they got homes to go to?
CUZ 1: Hey, Uncle, I got no money, I need clothes.
CUZ 2: I need food.
CUZ 3: I need medicine.
CUZ 4: I need car, Uncle.

TREVOR: Everyone who knows Albert… think they too good for the others. Don't have to work. Pastor worries, about the changes, about Albert… the future.
CUZ 1: Don't talk to me, talk to the hand. He's my uncle.
CUZ 2: He's not your uncle.
ALBERT: Ehh, shut up! Can't think 'ere!

They swear silently.

SCENE EIGHT: REX GETS MARRIED—SACRED GIFTS

Music: The Hermannsburg Choir can be heard under the following:

TREVOR: In the 1930s Rex and his fiancée Bernice live at the mission. The art is going well. Soon to be married in the little white stone chapel. Albert is away painting his country—beautiful Palm Valley. Big desert rains fall, lush and green, rockpools fill and flow. This is his mother's country, he's responsible for this place he loves.

And these are the crossover days. Albert has his *tjaarta*. [*We see him hunting with a spear.*] His *merra*. [*He shows his spear-thrower.*] His *urlpurrinya*. He hunts and paints his country.

He paints something special for his friend and his new bride. Wading into this waterhole, holding his picture in his teeth, he swims it through this strong water, walks long across hot sand. Carries it to that little church, to this friend, and his new wife, who are part of his country now.

Rex and Albert are kngwarra—like brothers. Rex has given Albert this watercolour, this new way out for his family. Albert has given him something… his tjurrunga. Sacred for him, which he would've kept hidden, precious, wrapped up, except now he walks both ways. The old men are proud of Albert, and they're strict with him. They know this Rex and Albert thing is special.

OLD ARANDA MAN: Rex, *pijai*! Battarbee, you belong to us now. *Aiyua Untjwaara era pitjika*… 'Untjwaara'. This is your name now.
REX: Thank you. And what does it mean, you know, just out of interest?
OLD ARANDA MAN: Means 'you belong to us, you brought us the colour blue'. *'Aiyua Untjwaara era pitjika.'* It means 'Old Heron'… like the bird. 'Old Heron Man has come!'

The ARANDA MAN *moves like a heron.*

REX: Old Heron, eh, thank you. Special name, is it? Sacred one, this bird, is it?

OLD ARANDA MAN: No, you just walk funny.

An air-raid siren is heard. Bombs dropping.

SCENE NINE: WORLD WAR TWO—NAZI

TREVOR: And then, 1942, the Japanese bomb Darwin. Maybe the Nazis are coming. American garrison there next to Alice. The Pastor, German, banished to Adelaide! Parliament in uproar!

OPPOSITION MEMBER: Who are those Germans in the desert? Mr Speaker?

GOVERNMENT MEMBER: Missionaries, Mr Speaker.

OPPOSITION MEMBER: Why did these Germans come here?

GOVERNMENT MEMBER: To save the Aboriginal people, and to speak on their behalf.

OPPOSITION MEMBER: Why are these German's stockpiling rice and wheat and vegetables?

GOVERNMENT MEMBER: Well, there's a severe drought, Mr Speaker, and the Government doesn't support the mission.

OPPOSITION MEMBER: Why have they got a radio transmitter?

GOVERNMENT MEMBER: Well, Flynn of the Inland gave it to them, for health reasons, I imagine.

OPPOSITION MEMBER: You imagine?! Can you assure Parliament that they are not Nazis and they are not sending messages to the Japanese? They know the whereabouts of the waterholes. What's to say they won't lead the enemy flooding across the country?! That Hermannsburg is run by Nazis! Mr Speaker.

TREVOR: And so a Captain Balfe was dispatched to search the mission, the Pastor banished. Battarbee, the dear old digger, who fought so valiantly, is installed as Resident Protector. The 'Old Waterbird' is left in charge of a bunch of German-speaking natives, in the middle of the desert. Every day he files a very important and secret report...

REX: [*on a shortwave radio*] Tuesday November 4, 1942. Hello, anybody there? This morning the enemy dive-bombed the vegie patch—bloody cockatoos into my cabbages again. Ummm, lots of flies about. Lovely clouds today—cumulus I think. Might go and do a spot of painting this arvo. So... Resident Protector, over and out.

SCENE TEN: CITIZENSHIP AND TAXES

TREVOR: After the war, 1948, Albert's exhibitions start to sell out before they open. Each picture, a hundred guineas now. His fame spreads overseas—fifty-seven paintings sold in Canada. Albert is a wealthy man... unheard of for a 'Black'. And so in recognition, the Government responds quickly. They decide he should be made a citizen—not so much because he's an important man, or the face of Australia internationally, or to redress the injustice—they decide he should become a citizen, because they want him to pay tax. See, you can't be taxed if you're a Ward of the State, if you are part of the 'flora and fauna'. You can't tax an animal, can you? So together, Rex and Albert try to stop this.

ALBERT: I don't want this citizen thing.

REX: Yeah, I know, mate.

ALBERT: This mob... you know what they'll ask me for.

ALBERT indicates the bottle.

REX: I know, we'll write a letter/

ALBERT: I'll have to buy it for them.

He indicates the bottle again.

REX: We'll go to Darwin. We'll appeal. We'll get them to understand.

TREVOR: Albert knows he'll be allowed to buy grog. If he's allowed to buy grog, he'll be humbugged. If he's humbugged, Aranda way, he'll have to buy it for others, he'll have to share it.

CUZ 1: Hey, Uncle, can you get some for me?

CUZ 2: Me two, Uncle, sorrow business/

CUZ 3: Hey, Uncle!

TREVOR: You see, Aranda way, Albert is not allowed to say no. But Government insists.

GOVERNMENT MAN: How good is this now, Albert? Quite a privilege. You'll be 'one of our first Aboriginal Citizens'. Your people will look up to you.

TREVOR: You know the first place the Welfare officers took him, when he became a citizen? To the pub. To buy him a beer. Too easy, mate. And... they tax him. Funny how they tax him, but they won't let him vote. It's not all bad, though. As a citizen Albert is allowed to live in town. In his own home. Doesn't have to be back on the mission before sundown anymore. Only thing is, his children, they aren't citizens, can't stay after dark, have to be back on the mish…

MAURICE: 'Night Mum.

RUBINA: 'Night Maurice.

MAISIE: 'Night Dad.

ALBERT: 'Night 'John Boy'. See you tomorrow.

TREVOR: It's not all bad. As a citizen he can buy land, for cattle station—security for family. Heart's a bit dickie these days. Albert's painting supports six hundred family, too hard. Needs to think smart. Good stockman, sons are too. Citizen now, paying tax.

ALBERT: We should buy property, get some cattle.

TREVOR: So, he and Rex apply to the Lands Department… buy his country back. Government agrees. Rex and Albert can't believe it, now things can change…

Music under: Reprise of 'Where the White Faced Cattle Roam'.

ALBERT: Good news, then? Rex?

REX: Yeah, ruddy terrific. Says here you can buy that land… I think. Except, um, wait a second… Seems like the boundaries have changed… a bit, or something.

TREVOR: Government reckon Albert can buy the land—'not a problem'—but they'll have to keep all the waterholes. For neighbouring graziers—white graziers, as it happens.

ALBERT: Iwana nana?

TREVOR: You see, Albert's land is just barren, useless desert.

REX: Well, mate, must be some mistake. We'll appeal. We'll go to Darwin, on the way to Sydney for that royal tour thing.

TREVOR: They want Albert to meet Australia's new queen.

ALBERT: Who this 'queen'?

TREVOR: Young Elizabeth, not long out of her teens—even *she's* heard of him. Government want to show him off… This Black man with 'actual talent'. 'Who'd have thought, eh?' Our first Black citizen… Our first Aboriginal listed in *Who's Who*. And so, to meet the Queen. Albert'll have to fly to Sydney from Darwin… So in Darwin he can appeal this Lands Deal. He'll get them to see, he'll get them to understand. With his little bit of English, this quietly spoken new citizen, this famous… taxpayer, this face of our country…

At the appeal:

ALBERT: Yes, sir... Thank you, sir... Um, it's about the waterholes, sir... for my family... I got eight children, sir... but sir... sir?

ALBERT *sits on the edge of a rock.*

TREVOR: Albert sits on the edge of Darwin Harbour, staring out to sea. First time he's seen the ocean, first time he's seen something this blue. First time he's felt it.

SCENE ELEVEN: THE SYDNEY TRIP

TREVOR: Albert the cameleer... now, Albert the jetsetter, Albert the pop star. Sydney Airport, mobbed by the curious, the paparazzi, well-wishers. Women faint. Intoxicated. Cameras follow his every move. Martin Place, press the flesh, crowds flock. Harbour cruise, sightseeing—Taronga Park Zoo. The Sydney 'art-er-rati' fawn, parading him. Society women touch him. So handsome, and exotic in red shirt 'n' cowboy hat.

SOCIALITE: Ahh, I shook Albert Namatjira's hand. Arahhh!

TREVOR: Invited out, black tie, Journalists Club. Had everything... except shoes. Take him by the hand... shopping for shoes. Wash his hard old gnarled feet. Nobody said anything, but he knew... poor fella.

ALBERT *washes his feet as the voice of a newsreel is heard.*

NEWSREEL: [*voice-over*] Albert Namatjira, the famous Aboriginal artist from Central Australia, caused a stir today at Sydney's famous zoo. Note the reaction of the animals to the proximity of a full-blooded native. Lions, tigers and particularly the apes sniff the air as they realise a descendant of the primeval jungle is among them. They jump up and down, hurling themselves against the bars of the cage, pick up handfuls of debris from the floor and throw it at their primitive cousin. Mahogany Man takes it all in his stride as he smiles for the camera.

ALBERT *wipes his feet. A shoebox is handed to him by a* NAMATJIRA FAMILY MEMBER *wearing a suit jacket.* ALBERT *tries on the shoes.*

TREVOR: How dignified he is, how quiet, how clever... To draw just like us... So famous now... William Dargie paints him for the Archibald.

As the music of 'God Save the Queen' plays, QUEEN ELIZABETH II *enters through the audience.*

Breath taken, our young Queen awards Albert the Coronation Medal… How deeply he bows to this little girl from London.
QUEEN ELIZABETH: Mr Namatjira? Or should I call you Albert? Named after my father, is that right?
ALBERT: I'm not so sure, ma'm/
QUEEN ELIZABETH: Prince Albert. Prince Albert Frederick Arthur George of Windsor. Or plain old George, which was rather fun, became King That rather spoilt things. Became 'King George the Sixth, by the Grace of God, of Great Britain, Ireland and the British Dominions beyond the Seas, King, Defender of the Faith, Emperor of India', which is rather a mouthful. Anyway, moving on, moving on…
ALBERT: Your Majesty…

DERIK *is reluctant to leave, enjoying his role as the* QUEEN.

TREVOR: Thank you, Derik. Derik…
DERIK: What?! It's not all about you, Trevor. You can have the stage and you know what, you can kiss my black ass.

The QUEEN *exits.*

TREVOR: Anyway, moving on, moving on…. Albert is invited to the State Theatre, variety show, there's a murmur of excitement as he enters. And then, as one, the audience stand, and on their feet, eyes turned toward him… a two-minute ovation. Why this ovation? What was it we were all yearning for in the cities? What was it about ourselves, that we saw as we stared through our little Namatjira windows, our cheap prints, over the mantelpiece, in our rows of fibro fifties homes in brand new Kirrawee? Who were we then, broken by war, ten-pound Poms, Italians with secret espresso machines, building the Snowy Mountain Scheme, proudly polishing those first FJ Holdens? What was it Rex and Albert were showing us in their friendship… some other Australia? A generous one? Not this one, the one we've found ourselves sliding into.

And so the paparazzi snap. Big news. *Sydney Morning Herald*: 'A black man we can be proud of'. And when news gets out that young Elizabeth loves her Namatjira painting, everyone wants one. Prices go through the roof—two hundred guineas! So famous now, our biggest companies want a piece of him, sponsor him, help him. Ampol gives him a shiny new truck… with his name on the side: 'ALBERT NAMATJIRA—ARTIST'.

REPORTER: So what do you think of your shiny new truck, Albert?
ALBERT: I like my truck.
REPORTER: Will it help you with your work?
ALBERT: It will help, yes.
REPORTER: Albert, over here. Do you have your driver's licence yet?
ALBERT: Licence? Who's this 'licence'?

SCENE TWELVE: TORN APART

TREVOR: Heading home in his truck. Celebrity, citizen, *Who's Who*, all the papers… rich, respected… in the city. At home, slave, humbugged for money, grog. Can't keep up. Shows others how to paint, others want what he has. Money starts trouble, mission falling apart. Pastor, retiring, now questions it all…
PASTOR: [*to himself*] Dear Lord, Verloren ihre Vergangenheit, aber nicht gefunden haben ihre Zukunft… They've lost their past, but haven't found their future.
CUZ 1: Hey, Uncle, picture for me. You gave him one! I need money.
TREVOR: Albert paints the hard parts, leaves the easy bits for them to fill.
CUZ 2: Hey, Uncle, I could paint, me. How you paint? Hey, Uncle!?
TREVOR: Without land, Albert is trying to survive. He sells his copyright, a dealer in Sydney… paid good money… Albert's idea, a friend of his, John Brackenridge. Now there are tea towels, biscuit tins, prints, placemats…
CUZ 3: Hey, Uncle, for my son, please, in jail there.
TREVOR: All gone… poor again. Only now, doesn't own his own image. Critics turn: 'It's not art… just a puppet', 'Stick to his primitive work'. They say, 'His friend Rex… ruined him!' In Sydney, that portrait of him, wins the Archibald… snapped up, big money. Albert all trussed up like a stuffed monkey. Charles Blackman says he has the saddest eyes of any man he's ever seen.

SCENE THIRTEEN: TAKE IT ALL

TREVOR *his takes shoes off and moves to a downstage rock.*
ALBERT: We see the way white people live, we want what they have. But Rex and I see what'll happen. All the time, asking for grog. I

can't say no. But Rex, he can't help me now… nobody can. I take my own pictures into town now.

The sound of a car.

TREVOR: Albert might have ten paintings ready at Ntaria… when he arrives in Alice Springs, only three left. One paid for the taxi, gave away three to family, one to the chemist, one for a flagon. Famous now, everyone in Alice knows what his pictures are worth. Rex tells him…
REX: Why give them away for a flagon worth threepence?
ALBERT: They asked nice way.
TREVOR: Albert paints his beloved Ntaria, MacDonnell Ranges. 'Caterpillar Dreaming'—two hundred guineas—gone. Treadmill…
CUZ 1: Please, Uncle?
REX: Slave… flagon…
CUZ 1: Please, Uncle?
ALBERT: Go on, take it…! Get out of it…! Take the lot of it!

SCENE FOURTEEN: HIS FATHER PASSES AWAY

TREVOR *sits in his chair, modelling for the artist.*

The lines of ALBERT *and the* SPIRIT OF ALBERT'S FATHER *overlap as the same thought.*

SPIRIT: *Yinga itjama Albert-anha.*
ALBERT: My name is not Albert.
SPIRIT: *Rretyna nuka itja Namatjira.*
ALBERT: My name is not Namatjira.
SPIRIT: *Rretnya nuka itja Ilia.*
ALBERT: My name was Elea.
SPIRIT: *Rretnya arrpunha nuka nama, Tunungka.*
ALBERT: My name was Tonanga.
SPIRIT: *Kaarta nukanhaka rretnya itja Namatjira nama.*
ALBERT: Namatjira is not my father's name.
SPIRIT: *Ekura rretnya itja Jonathan.*
ALBERT: His name was not Jonathan.
SPIRIT: *Kaarta nuka kala yarraka.*
ALBERT: My father is finished now.

SPIRIT: Rretnya arrunha karta…
ALBERT: Died with the wrong name.

The SPIRIT *sings 'Kunpinya' under the following:*

That Flying Ant Dreaming, he was. [*He shows us.*] This Carpet Snake Dreaming, I am. [*He shows us.*] Where did I go? I am not a man. Who am I? I could tell you a story… Feathered Serpent… *Erintja*… Devil Dog, Eagle-men of *Alkutnama*, Old Man and His Six Sons, the *Namatuna*. What story should I tell you? The Jesus story? The painting story? What story do you want from me? Maybe I have no story now. I'll tell you the story everyone wants to hear. The only story whitefellas seem to remember.

SCENE FIFTEEN: POLICE

ALBERT: Listen. [*He listens.*] Hear that? *Raberaba*—good fella. Little bit drunk, sounds like. Out there at Morris Soak. [*He listens.*] Hear that? Woman there, Pitjantjatjara. Where did he get his flagon from? [*He listens.*] *Raberaba*… hear him? Angry now… drunk, blind drunk. Wants that one. [*He listens.*] Have to be a citizen to buy grog.

The sound of fire.

Raberaba has that Pitjanjatjara woman now. He wants her. Angela, is that her name? Fighting him off… too strong for her. [*He listens.*] Hear that? Big fire near… too near. [*He listens.*] Hear that? Getting what he wants. [*He listens.*] Hear that? Club now… rolling… in that fire… Angela… finished. Tomorrow, he won't remember. Police looking, wanting answers. Only one citizen round here.

SCENE SIXTEEN: THE LIGHT FADING

ALBERT *stands before the court alone. Handcuffed. Head bowed. His suit tatty. He looks older, sicker.*

MAGISTRATE: Albert Namatjira, this represents a serious betrayal of the trust placed in you…

TREVOR: Mr Dodds, Senior Magistrate presiding. Albert says nothing—shamed, humiliated, haggard, drawn, blue. Why have people turned on him? Left him?

MAGISTRATE: You abused the privilege of citizenship, you supplied liquor to a Ward of the State. Your actions led to the rape and murder of an innocent woman. And, although you weren't present, as an example to your people, I sentence you to six months hard labour. All rise.

Music starts.

DERIK *sings 'Abide With Me' under the following:*

DERIK: [*sung, in Aranda, under*]
*Etatha nuka paarrpa yarrama,
Aalhak' arrkana ipmintj-errama
Ingkarrakima Ithulth-erramanga
Untarrpa itja kngartiwulhama.*

*Nukanga itj' empunhai, Ingkaartai
Kangkintja pula, atampa turta
Nuka-lela ekaarrkarranha nai
Kurtungurl' etnaka-lela ngerra!*

TREVOR: Albert, our number one man, taken—old man with a bad heart—under escort from the court to the jail. Word filters out slowly to the city. Amid murmurs of 'I told you so', an outcry in the media: 'Through this disgraceful court action Albert Namatjira has gone from Government House to Government Dump... and now finds himself imprisoned.' Eventually the court says he can serve out the rest of his time in Papunya. Taken under escort, in his shiny green ute. That old Carpet Snake is weak. Spent. For old Elea... everything feels blue. Tonanga can't paint. See him sitting there, staring into space, holding a brush, can't paint. His country gone now... the light fading... slowly singing himself to death.

It's hot in Alice, at the funeral, too hot to wait for family. In the lane behind the hospital, Rubina in a taxi, a truckload of people. And so, between taxi and hearse, his old friend, the Pastor, holds a short service... in Aranda and English.

TREVOR *takes off Albert's shirt and undershirt and folds them into a pile.*

KEVIN NAMATJIRA *brings Albert's hat and places it on top of the clothing, on a rock.*

Silent prayer.

The singing music finishes.

The NAMATJIRA FAMILY ARTISTS *return to their picture making.*

TREVOR *returns to sit on the portrait chair.*

And then the hearse is gone, past the gates of the prison, where we held him. This great man we adored—used, abused and then abandoned. This first one… gone, into the blue.

The lights pause on the portrait, then snap to black.

THE END

Ngapartji Ngapartji
written for Trevor Jamieson (Pitjantjatjara)

Trevor Jamieson (left) and Yumi Umiumare in Ngapartji Ngapartji, *2009*
Big hART *and Belvoir production at Belvoir St Theatre in Sydney.*
(Photo: Heidrun Löhr)

Ngapartji ngapartji: I give you something, you give me something

Big hART produced the first full-length season of *Ngapartji Ngapartji* for the Melbourne International Arts Festival in October 2006, and then for the Perth International Arts Festival in 2007. Following is the list of key participants who created the show:

PRINCIPAL PERFORMER & CO-CREATOR	Trevor Jamieson
OTHER PERFORMERS	Jarmen Jamieson
	Tomoko Yamasaki
	Lex Marinos
	Saira Luther
	Julie Miller
	Elton Wirri
	Mervin Adamson
	Yumi Umiumare
MUSICIANS	Damian Mason
	Andrew McGregor
	Beth Sometimes
CHOIR	Pitjantjatjara women

Writer/Director, Scott Rankin
Set & Costume Design, Genevieve Dugard
Lighting Design, Neil Simpson
Musical Director, Damian Mason
Choreographer, Yumi Umiumare
AV Design, Cicada + Tim Webster; Olaf Meyer
Language Content Producer & Video Artist, Suzy Bates
Creative Producer, Alex Kelly
Production Manager, Mel Robertson
Stage Manager, Jess Smithett
Assistant Stage Manager/Ceramicist, Zoe Churchill
Choir Co-ordinator, Beth Sometimes
Researcher, Melanie Gillbank
Associate Producer, GNG Productions

Language Teachers: Pantjiti McKenzie, Jennifer Mitchell, Lorna Wilson

Language Tutors and Workshop Participants: Deanne Gillen, Julie Coulthard, Julie Miller, Elton Wirri, Sandy Brokus-Abbott, Alana Kelly, Delaine Singer, Agnes Yamma, Belinda Swan, Janice Stanley, Sarah Lee Langois, Melissa Kingsley, Roshelle Minutjukur, Bianca Forrest, Mikailah Abbott, Wanyima Richards, Carly Miller, Darlene Buzzacott, Mervin Adamson, Lily Jack, Conway Ginger, Nathanial Garrawurra, Cyril McKenzie, Tjinkuma Dunn, Aaron Dixen, Sadie Richards, Gabrielle Kulitja.

Pitjantjatjara Translations: Thomas Holder and Beth Sometimes.

Cultural advisors: senior Pitjantjatjara women.

Acknowledgements: Trevor Jamieson and the Jamieson family for sharing their story and Alex Kelly as Creative Producer.

CAST

Performers:
- TREVOR JAMIESON
- JARMEN JAMIESON (JANGALA)
- LEX MARINOS
- SAIRA LUTHER
- JULIE MILLER
- ELTON WIRRI
- SADIE RICHARDS
- BELINDA ABBOTT
- YUMI UMIUMARE
- LORNA WILSON
- NAJEEBA AZIMI

Choir:
- PANTJITI MCKENZIE
- JENNIFER MITCHELL
- IRIS AJAX
- JANET INYIKA
- IMUNA KENTA
- MAKINTI MINUTJUKUR
- PANTJITI LEWIS
- AMANYI DORA HAGGIE
- NAMI KULYURU
- RENITA STANLEY
- RHODA TJITAYI
- MELISSA THOMPSON

Musicians:
- DAMIAN MASON
- ANDREW MCGREGOR
- BETH SOMETIMES

The cast members play numerous characters throughout the performance.

CHARACTERS

Main Characters:

TREVOR JAMIESON
PANTJITI MCKENZIE and AMANYI HAGGIE, Pitjantjatjara elders
TJAMU JACK JAMIESON, Trevor's grandfather
ARNOLD JAMIESON, Tjamu Jack's son
ARNOLD'S MOTHER, Trevor's grandmother
MR STEWART
SOLDIER
JARMEN JAMIESON (JANGALA)
GAIL, Trevor's mother
TJAMU HUGHIE WINDLASS, goes to London to fight for compensation
CHOIR

Other Characters:

BRITISH EXPLORER
MRS HAZEL BLAIR
TV ANNOUNCER
TJILPI (OLD MAN)
JUDGE, in London

A NOTE ABOUT THE STAGING

The performance space is defined by a large copper-coloured shell which stands towards the rear of the stage. It is angled in such a way that performers can stand on it, climb over it, or be concealed behind it.

The floor of the stage is covered in black sand.

There is a delicate sculpted metal screen, above the back of the stage, upon which various projections appear.

Towards the back of the stage, stage right, sits a choir of Pitjantjatjara women. They stand when they sing, afterwards resuming their seats and becoming witnesses to the authenticity of the story as it unfolds.

Some sections of dialogue (and song lyrics) appear in the text in Pitjantjatjara language with English translation in brackets after. Both the Pitjantjatjara and English text are spoken (or sung) in performance.

True to the genesis of this project, this script uses the names of family members and original cast members.

The performance style is informal and varies from night to night. There is improvisation and byplay amongst the cast in some scenes.

SCENE ONE

SCREEN: *A moon slowly rises for twenty minues as the audience enters.*
MUSICIANS *enter—a Japanese flute plays, with guitar.*
The house lights dim.
SCREEN: *A film of* JANGALA *(Trevor's brother) running in the desert.*
TREVOR *enters. He watches the film.*

TREVOR: *Munga kuwarina mukuringangi pitja palyantjikitja ngayuku malanypa Jangalanyatjara.* [For tonight, I was just going to make a film about my brother Jangala.] *Paluṟu pukuḻpa nyinanyi putingka...* [Jangala is happy in the bush...] but he spends a lot of time in prison. I worry: *Mununa pulkaṟa kulini tjinguṟu kuwari paluṟu iluku.* [He may not be here long.] Finished... I wanted to make a film about him... but then my family turned up... So we're gonna be here for a very long time.

We hear the CHOIR *singing offstage. They enter, singing.*

SONG: *'Walytja'* ('Family')
CHOIR: [*sung*]
    Tjamu, kami,
    Mama ngunytju,
    Kuṯa kangkuṟu, kulilaya,
    Nyangatja tjukurpa nyuntumpa ngalimpa
    Nyaakun kuliṟa wantinyi nyangatja
TREVOR: I better introduce you to my *walytja*, my family.

He introduces some of the Pitjantjatjara cast.

I'll hand you over to my sister Makinti, and my mothers, Pantjiti and Jenny. *Wai Makinti, palya, nyuranya?*
MAKINTI: [*to* TREVOR] *Uwa palya?*
TREVOR: *Uwa.*

TREVOR *drifts to the back as* MAKINTI *teaches the audience some words.*

MAKINTI: *Wai.* '*Wai*' is a way of getting attention... polite way.

Palya.
Uwa palya.
Now we're going to teach you a simple song: 'Heads and Shoulders, Knees and Toes'.

SCREEN: *The words come up.*

    MAKINTI *goes through each word and gets the audience to repeat it. She explains each word by pointing to a part of the body.*

MAKINTI: *Kata. Alipiri. Muti. Tjina. Pina. Kuru. Winpinpi. Mulya.*

    The CHOIR *sing first, then encourage the audience to join in.*

SONG: *'Kata, Alipiri, Muti, Tjina'* ('Heads and Shoulders, Knees and Toes')

CHOIR: [*sung*]
    Kata, alipiri, muti, tjina,
    Muti tjina, muti tjina,
    Kata alipiri, muti, tjina,
    Pina, kuru, winpinpi, mulya

CHOIR & AUDIENCE: [*sung together*]
    Kata, alipiri, muti, tjina,
    Muti tjina, muti tjina,
    Kata alipiri, muti, tjina,
    Pina, kuru, winpinpi, mulya

    The CHOIR *improvise getting the audience to stand up and sing, dividing them into sections and conducting each group—gently as if with young children in school.*

    TREVOR *comes forward again.*

TREVOR: *Nganampa walytja pulka nyinanyi ka nyurampa kulinytja kutjupa tjuku-tjuku.* [Our family, our *waltyja*, is bigger than how most people might think of family.]

    He introduces the non-Pitjantjatjara cast members.

This is Saira, some of her family come from India, she's *waltyja*.

SAIRA: *Namaste.*

TREVOR: This is Lex, he's from Greece…

LEX: *Yasis.*

TREVOR: … and Wagga Wagga.

LEX: G'day.
TREVOR: This is Andrew, our brother. He's from Melbourne…
ANDREW: Hi.
TREVOR: This is Damien.
DAMIEN: Hi.
TREVOR: This is Beth. She's from New Zealand and Ernabella.
This is Yumi, she's from Japan, we call her 'sister', she's from Japan.
YUMI: *Konnichiwa.*
TREVOR: *Watytja*, [family,] is big for us, Some nights we sing the *walytja* song in a different language. Maybe we could sing in Greek or maybe Japanese. Yumi, how does this song go in your language?

YUMI *sings in Japanese.*

SCENE TWO

SCREEN: *The shadow image of a crow appears.*

TREVOR: 1957… Adelaide… in a schoolyard, *tjintungka*, [in the sun,] a crate of small school milk bottles sits warming. Silver tops glint. In a silver gum, a glistening *kaanka*… [crow…] *parpakani,* [leaps to flight,] lands on the crate, and pecks a hole in the glinting foil. *Paluru nyanganyi,* [She looks,] sips, looks, sips again.
Young and black and silky and sexy and *wati uwankara palumpa mukuringanyi.* [every male wants her.]
Soon, her nest is full, a hungry brood, and soon, *manngu tjaangka,* [on the edge of the nest,] first flight beckons her young ones. She watches as they *parpakara* [leap into flight] and then… plummet, stunned, *ilunyi.* [dying.] Each born weak-boned. *Paluru purkarangku altinyi…* [She calls quietly…] *nyangangka kutjuparinyi…* [something is happening here…]

He slides down the copper shell.

Music to 'Once in a Lifetime' (a Talking Heads song) begins.

1950s, 1960s, 1970s, Australian scientists steal the bones of dead children during autopsy, white children, black children, without asking. They grind them into powder, for analysis… Why?

He takes clay dust from a bowl.

Just twenty years ago, 1986, *ngayuku walytja latjawana...* [the last of my family...] They were still living in the desert. *Tjana piṟanpa tjuṯa kuwaripatjarangku nyangu...* [They saw white people for the first time...]
Nyangangka kutjuparinyi. [Something is happening here.]
JANGALA *appears ominous in silhouette upstage. He is running on the spot.*
He continues the run or lift weights throughout the show as a faint presence.
TREVOR *and the* CHOIR *sing* 'Wantiriyalani' *(a Pitjantjatjara language version of 'Once in a Lifetime').*

SCENE THREE

TREVOR: 1841. Ooldea, South Australia... *manta unngu wanampi kunkunpa ngarinyi.* [under the ground here, Wanampi is sleeping.] *Liru puḻka...* [Big snake...] As long as we look after Ooldea, *liru paluṟu ngariku.* [that snake will sleep.] As long as Wanambi sleeps, *kunkunpa ngariku, kapi rawa ngariku ooldeala.* [there'll always be *kapi*—water in Ooldea.] But, shhh, something is happening...

As both pony and rider, TREVOR *performs dressage.*

British explorers, on their lovely British ponies.

The pony does a poo, circles around and slips in it.

BRITISH EXPLORER: [*voice-over*] Oh, bother! This wretched spinifex has ripped the pony's legs to smithereens... If we are to tame this desert country, we'll need a tenacious beast that can regulate the moisture in its poo... I know... camels! We need camels! Afghanees! Bring 'em here by boat, down past Christmas Island, put 'em in the desert... Transport industry... Just like Lindsay Fox.

SCREEN: *An advertising slogan:'You are passing another camel'.*

Afghan music plays under.

TREVOR *plays* TJAMU *('grandfather'), hunting.*

TREVOR: Near Ooldea, my *tjamu* is hunting. He sees this *kuka malikitja.* [strange creature.] See, *nguṉti waṟa inyutjara...*

He shows a long neck.
[*Speaking again*] ... *tjunta nyurka, wara mulapa.*
He shows long legs.
And this man, with big head all wound round, *paluru tjantarngaranyi.* [kneeling on a rug.]
Ka ngayuku tjamungku rawangku nyanganyi, [And my pop is looking and looking,] from behind a *punu.* [a bush.] *Paluru putu kulini.* [He doesn't know what to think.] And then the man sees him and he goes: [*making a gun with his hands*] 'Boom'...
A bullet passes close to his head.
... *nyanganyi,* [looking,] *munu nyanganyi,* [and looking,] and: [*making a gun again*] 'Boom'.
Looks again, and my *tjamu paluru kulinyi kuwari paluru iluku.* [thinks he's going to die there.] So he *wakanu palunya.*
He throws a spear.
Nyangangka kutjuparinyi... [Something is happening here...]
More of these strange men keep coming,
Hundreds of them, Afghans,
Building mosques, in our country
Facing Mecca every day,
Marrying my *walytja*,
Building snake tracks across my country,
And when these Afghans have finished their work...
This big silver *liru* is coming, breathing *puyu*,
And these white ghost people live inside it like maggots.
And the *liru* stops at Ooldea and they lean out the windows and wave to you,
And if you do a bit of this...
He becomes a kangaroo.
... and you do a bit of this...
He becomes malu [*emu*]*.*
... they'll clap and give you money... bit like tonight really.

SCENE FOUR

The CHOIR *sing a reprise of part of* 'Wantiriyalani' *('Once in a Lifetime').*

TREVOR: *Ngura wirunya nganampa.* [Oldea was a special place for us.] *Kala ngura panya atunmara kanyinma, palu kapikula mukuringanyi. Kapi wiyangka witu-witu nganampa ngaranyi.* [We look after it because we need that water, it was lovely there, like an oasis, like a resort for us—for holidays, relieve the stress, because life was hard back then.]
[*While hunting with a spear*] See, *nganana anangu kutjupa,* [we're a different mob,] we didn't use trucks to bring food to where we live, we'd *para-ankupai* [move around] to where that food was.

He physicalises a kangaroo. Throws a spear, is speared and then carries the kangaroo, lights a fire, cooks it, as if waiting for a microwave 'ding'.

A microwave 'dings'.

Wirunya, [Lovely,] see now, *wati tjilpi munu minyma pampa kuranyi ngaranyi.* [elders first.] Most people want lean meat, but we need the fatty stuff, the tail, mmm, cholesterol. Mmm…
Hunting in the city happens different way, you need a special hunting suit, [*trying one on*] drop the *tjitji tjuta* [kids] off some place, climb in the *tjuni* [belly] of a big silver *liru* to the city, [*getting on a train, holding a strap, etc.*] and sit all day in a small room, staring at a flashing box. [*At a desk*] If you do this for days… money in a wall for you.

The sound of an ATM dispensing cash.

And then, you can go to a gourmet butcher [*choosing carefully*] and buy a small piece of lean organic *kuka malu,* [kangaroo steak,] which you take home and cook, on a campfire that comes to your home in long pipes.

The sound of lighting gas and cooking.

When we were *kukaku ngurini,* [finding food,] we'd move across different country. We had to be careful *tjinguru anangu kutjupa nyakuku,* [might meet new people,] and you have to *anangu pulkaku kuntarikuntjaku,* [show respect to the most senior person,] or they could *nyuntunya wakalku.* [spear you.] So the polite thing to do was to smell them.

He smells men in the front row.

This one, doesn't smell, *wati tjuku-tjuku*... [he's a nobody...] this fella's a bit on the nose... but this one...

He holds his nose.

... *paluru panti una! Wati pulka mulapa.* [Very important man.]

He shakes hands with the important man.

All this was *witu-witu,* [hard work,] *tjuni kuralpai* [we'd get stressed out] too, so every year, for thousands of years, *munula alataiku ankupai,* [we'd go on holiday,] to where that snake was, Ooldea Resort. *Tjukurlangka tjurpipai, munu kuka pulka ngalkulpai,* [Plenty of swimming, food,] emu, *malu, maku,* quandong, pizza, smorgasbord.

He lazes back.

We'd lie around the pool, *tjitji tjuta inkanyi miri wiru nikitipurunpa mantjini*— [kids playing, we're getting up a nice tan—] obviously. Bit like Port Douglas, eh... *Kuka, mai palu mani wiya*... [Good service, free food, activities...] *kimi inkapai, kali waninyi, nyiri mamaku nintini,* [badminton, Bible study, boomerang throwing... naked].

He throws a boomerang, miming with his forearm that he is naked and his penis is flopping around.

Trying to catch the boomerang, it hits an audience member in the head. He pulls the boomerang out of their skull.

So there are still big mobs of us *putingka nyinanyi munu atunymara kanyiningi manta wirungka* [out in the bush looking after country] but these people want all of us to live under tin roof. My tjamu, Tjamu Jack Jamieson, he comes and goes with his wife, and now she's this way for my father. They want Tjamu Jack to come in to the mission so they leave food, clothes, for us to find... bit like Hansel and Gretel.

TREVOR *exits behind the copper shell.*

The women of the CHOIR *stand.*

SONG: *'Wanalku Wanalku'* (a Pitjantjatjara language version of the hymn 'I Will Follow Jesus'.

CHOIR: [*sung*]
>*Wanalku wanalku ngayu Jesus wanalku*
>*Nyangakutu palakutu ngayu palunya wanalku*
>*Wanalku wanalku ngayu Jesus wanalku*
>*Nyangakutu palakutu ngayu wanalku.*

>TREVOR *enters wearing an old-style woman's apron as the* CHOIR *sit.*

TREVOR: But the men didn't know which clothes to wear—start of the fine Australian tradition of cross-dressing.
They give us new names and date of birth… kind of them. We got 'Jameson'… which is the traditional Pitjantjatjara name for… 'whiskey'… I think. And they give us lovely new songs…

>*The women of the* CHOIR *resume the hymn.*

CHOIR: [*sung*]
>*Wanalku wanalku ngayu Jesus wanalku*
>*Nyangakutu palakutu ngayu palunya wanalku*
>*Wanalku wanalku ngayu Jesus wanalku*
>*Nyangakutu palakutu ngayu wanalku.*

TREVOR: [*sung over the* CHOIR]
I'm too young to march in the infantry,
Ride in the cavalry,
Shoot the artillery,
I'm too young to fly over land and sea,
But I'm in the Lord's army…

>SAIRA *continues to sing the text.*

SAIRA: [*sung*]
I'm too young to march in the infantry,
Ride in the cavalry,
Shoot the artillery,
I'm too young to fly over land and sea,
But I'm in the Lord's army…

TREVOR: So during what you call the 1940s, my *tjamu*, Jack Jamieson, and his wife walk in and out from Ooldea Mission, to the *ngura panya paluru atunymara kanyintjaku,* [country he has to look after,] the nation he wants his children to be born into, Spinifex Nation… so they'll look after it… and our country is the size of your Great Britain, it's hard work to look after… and then, unknown to us *nyangangka kutjuparinyi…* [something is happening here…]

SONG: *'Urungka Tjarpara-Tjarpara'* ('The Swimming Song'—a song for children)

CHOIR: [*sung*]
    Urungka tjarpara-tjarpara
    Urungka tjarpara-tjarpara
    Nyiingangkunitju kunta kuntani
    Nyiingangkunitju kunta kuntani.

SCENE FIVE

Clapsticks continue to beat under with other music and sound effects.
The Japanese dancer/speaker, YUMI, *slowly enters—Bhuto movement.*
TREVOR *enters over the top of the shell from behind.*
Dance and text are simultaneous throughout this scene.

TREVOR: 1940s,
    That nation you call America,
    Apple-pie young men are dying,
    All-American kitchen-sink tears, fall,
    Crying-apron-string-strong mums beg,
    Arms industry on the ball,
    Beckon big-brained, pink-skinned scientists,
    Hunkered down in bunker, in desert deep, till
    An atom spat miracle secrets, and split,
    An answer to mamma's prayer at president's feet…

    The CHOIR *resumes* '*Urungka Tjarpara-Tjarpara*' (*'The Swimming Song'*).

SCREEN: *Abstract textures and random images of war.*

TREVOR: 1940s,
    Nation you call Britain,
    On the beaches fight,
    Decent men… skittish, shocked by shell, fall,

Dead, in the dead night of dawn,
Navy sinking, economy on the brink,
Stiff upper lips tremble,
British mums blinking tears,
Whimper for bygone glory days of empire,
Now with this defeated king,
She too, has her best scientists thinking...

> *The* CHOIR *continues* 'Urungka Tjarpara-Tjarpara' (*'The Swimming Song'*).

TREVOR: 1940s,
That giant you call Russia,
Stung, lumbers from bearish sleep to action stations,
Western Front minions march, in dying millions,
White snow red, as red army bleeds,
A cold new world order,
Built on her teenage dead.

> *The Japanese version of 'Kata, Alipiri, Muti, Tjina' ('Head and Shoulders') runs under* TREVOR*'s dialogue.*

YUMI & SAIRA: [*together, sung in Japanese*]
    Heads and shoulders, knees and toes, knees and toes,
    Heads and shoulders, knees and toes...

ACTOR: The dying days of World War Two, Japan... A grandfather, watches his granddaughter play in the garden. A nursery rhyme... The morning air is crisp.

> *The Japanese singing continues under the text.*

YUMI & SAIRA: [*together, sung in Japanese*]
    Heads and shoulders, knees and toes, knees and toes,
    Heads and shoulders, knees and toes...

LEX: High above, the drone of a silver bird. He thinks of his time in the Japanese Navy. World War One. The covering fire they gave the Australian diggers landing on the shore, in a long-forgotten, bungled skirmish, some place called Gallipoli. Years ago, he rubs the scar on his shattered leg and smiles at her simple song.

> YUMI *speaks Japanese while dancing.* SAIRA *translates some of the words in English under.*

SAIRA: [*translating from the Japanese*]
    My daughter playing,
    She hears a crow calling,
    Cargo doors sigh…

    The sound of a bomb exploding.

Flash of blue wind,
Flattened, pushed to ground,
Houses sucked high,
Fall as shrapnel rain,
I wipe my face, I
Wipe my face off,
Lace skin dripping,
Calling her,
My daughter wanders,
Without lips,
With no face,
Tongue burnt,
My daughter wonders who calls her.
How quiet it is,
Rain, black, falling,
Water sucked from river,
Flame crackles,
Fires roar,
My daughter, walking,
Cool river, calling,
Tsurumi Bridge,
I follow.
People,
Not people,
Pumpkin heads, zombies,
See cool water, jump from bridge,
Into water, boiling,
Fish float, cooked.
In the water,
A woman with no face, reflected,
Me.

TREVOR: 1946,
    America's,
    Shiny new big-boy toy,
    Turns heads of other nations,
    Green with envy at piles at civilian skin peeling,
    From shapeless slant eyes swollen shut,
    This favourite new toy,
    A present for America's mums
    Who with open arms and plump scones,
    Welcome home America's sons,
    And nations, envious… haggle, jostle, wangling, and,
    Make haste to deploy,
    This toy for melting faces…
       YUMI *speaks in Japanese.*
LEX: [*translating from the Japanese*]
    By the river,
    My daughter,
    Feeds ducks, skin,
    Skin, from her face.
    Dead ducks.
    From my cheeks,
    Droplets,
    Like crystal, weep,
    Drip from chin,
    Thirsty, I lick,
    My head swells,
    A pumpkin, crust cracking,
    People wander from city,
    To cool country,
    The crippled lead the blind,
    Shuffling.

    That day,
    Camped by our river,
    No-one cried,
    No feelings,
    People died,

Nerves ending.
That day,
Sky dark at noon,
Beside the ducks in the Spiderwart reeds.
By our poisoned river,
My poisoned daughter,
Crying, I, drown her,
And watch soldiers throw her body on a funeral fire.

TREVOR: And World War Two over,
The nation you call Britain, broken,
No money, steel, ships, coal, a token empire…
No more colonies and clubs, cigars and slaves,
Or Far-East ice teas and salad days,
Her birthright a token,
On her knees to the US, begging,
Give us these dirt-cheap secrets, please…
America, the tease, cries,
Too much MI5-old-boy-public-school sleaze,
Britain rife with Russian spies,
Every good man, left standing,
Is on his knees, with upper lip stiff,
As she turns to her faithful colony,
To be appeased… Mr Menzies,
Can we test this thing in your desert… thank you.
And in the nation you call Australia,
Red perils, yellow perils, red perils, yellow perils, red
Under every red-brick suburban yellow-stained saggy bed,
Your prime minister, Menzies, running scared,
Needs a frightening friend, says,
'Please, test a Cold War toy or two',
There's nothing out there,
In Spinifex country,
Just flora and fauna at the world's end…

The CHOIR *stand.*

SONG: *'Kata, Alipiri, Muti, Tjina'* ('Heads and Shoulders, Knees and Toes') reprise

CHOIR: [*sung*]
>Kata, alipiri, muti, tjina,
>Muti tjina, muti tjina,
>Kata alipiri, muti, tjina,
>Pina, kuru, winpinpi, mulya.

ACTOR: In the shadow of World War Two, in the north of England, a young woman, Hazel Blair, gives birth to a son, Tony. They move to South Australia. Hazel Blair looks after young Tony. The war is over. Life is good. They play outdoors in the clean Australian air… A *Kaanka*, watches, curious, as they sing.

SAIRA: [*sung as* MRS BLAIR]
>Heads and shoulders, knees and toes,
>Knees and toes,
>Heads and shoulders knees and toes…

The Japanese dance ends.

The CHOIR *walk forward singing.*

SCENE SIX

TREVOR: [*breaking the sombre mood*] Hands up any grandfathers here tonight… We call you *tjamu*… Any grandmothers?… We call you *kami*.

He goes through the 'Walytja' ('Family') song, teaching the audience each word.

So what do you think the word for 'father' is?… *Mama*.

He continues to teach the words to the song. Then:

Uwa, inma now. [We're going to sing it now.] You want more lesson?

They sing.

TREVOR & AUDIENCE: [*sung together*]
>Tjamu, kami,
>Mama ngunytju,
>Kuta kangkuru, kulilaya,
>Nyangatja tjukurpa nyuntumpa ngalimpa
>Nyaakun kulira wantini nyangatja.

TREVOR: [*to* PANTJITI] Was that alright?… [*To the audience*] You want to sing on your own?

The audience try their best.

AUDIENCE: [*sung*]
Tjamu, kami,
Mama ngunytju,
Ku<u>t</u>a kangku<u>r</u>u, kulilaya,
Nyangatja tjukurpa nyuntumpa ngalimpa
Nyaakun kuli<u>r</u>a wantini nyangatja.

TREVOR: *Palya? Palya.* [Very good.]

The CAST *applaud the audience.*

Over time, there have been a lot of Afghans in Australia, who came here and helped and married into our people and became family... before meeting white people. It's easy to forget that... Saira, what does this sound like in Afghan language?

SAIRA *sings the song as the* CHOIR *return to their seats.*

SCREEN: *A shadow image of country.*

TREVOR *creates a tree and a rock pool.*

He carries a baby boy.

YOUNG PEOPLE *create a white line with powder across the stage in a line of light as* TREVOR *begins the following.*

TREVOR: *Tjanpiku ngurangka,* [Spinifex country,] at start of a cold war. *Pu<u>n</u>u watangka tjuku<u>r</u>la itingka,* [Under a tree by a rock pool,] in the cool of the evening, a baby boy, Arnold, son of Jack Jamieson, takes his first breaths of air in his country. He is healthy, his mother is healthy...

He kneels down at a small pile of white bones.

JULIE *walks across along the path created by the powder.*

Next day, they walk to new hunting grounds. *Ngura panya palula kuwari, para-nga<u>r</u>anyi* [The country she walks across] *ngura palumpa, palumpa katjangku ngula kanyintjaku.* [is the country her baby boy will be responsible for.] Babies have always been born into this responsibility. As she carries her new son, *palumpa nguntjungku palunya inma inka<u>r</u>a ngaritjunu...* [his *nguntju*, my grandmother, lulls him to sleep with a song...]

JULIE *finishes walking during the following song.*

TREVOR *is nursing the baby as* TJAMU JACK. *He stands.*

ALL: [*sung*]
Tjamu, kami,
Mama ngunytju,
Kuṯa kangkur̲u, kulilaya,
Nyangatja tjukurpa nyuntumpa ngalimpa
Nyaakun kulir̲a wantini nyangatja.

The sound of a truck is heard far off.

SCREEN: MR STEWART *appears in silhouette.*

MR STEWART: *Wai tjuu, palya. Nyuntu ankunytjaku* [You gotta leave] *kura palyalpaingkatawara* [to avoid bad] *irati kura mulapa,* [poison, truly bad,] *puyu kuramulapa.* [smoke, truly bad.] *Mula-mulan̲anta wangkanyi.* [Genuine, you talking.] *Ara, ara tjuu.* [Go, go, old friend.] We have to get out now, to new *ngura, upurlupurlila nguraritja.*

TJAMU JACK *is listening to* MR STEWART.

The sound of a plane flying over scares him.

JULIE *enters and stands next to the copper shell, afraid.*

TREVOR: *Upurlupurlila ngurratja...* home of the Tadpole... Four hundred and forty-two miles west. Cundalee. Without his country, *wiyangka, palur̲u wiya ngar̲aku.* [baby Arnold will have nothing, he'll be nothing.] And they have to leave straight away because the government thinks there is no-one out there and *wati stewartu tjamu jacknya munu an̲angu tjuṯa wangkangu ankuntjaku.* [Mr Stewart needs Tjamu Jack to convince the others to leave.] He has to get his wife on the truck... *Ka Arnoldku nguntju nguluntju kuwari ngar̲anyi...* [But Arnold's mother is scared...] she's never seen a truck.

JULIE *lies down in the shell.*

Tjana Arnoldaku ngura wantikatingu, [So they left the country given to Arnold,] his nation. And his mother lay on the floor of the truck whimpering, vomiting, holding on tight to baby Arnold, and she's thinking... *Paluru pur̲unypa...* 'Same as it ever was, same as it ever was...'

SCENE SEVEN

SOLDIER: After World War Two… they called for volunteers… Wouldn't tell us what for, but the money was surprisingly good. I was off like a shot.

TREVOR: *Ngayuku walytjangku kulira tjina nyukula munu palulangurula kumpinu.* [Sometimes my family'd hear them or see their tracks and we'd hide.]

SOLDIER: We arrived in this secret location… middle of the desert. They'd thrown up this city. Knew something was on then. Soldiers, scientists and civies racing around. Seventeen thousand of us went through that place. Maralinga.

TREVOR: *Ngananа tjitji tjutanya kumpitjunkula watuku pitingka munula puli katukutu waningu tjulpu tjilpa wati-ankunyangka.* [When the silver birds'd flew over and we'd hide the children down wombat holes and throw stones at the sky].

 TREVOR *drifts off.*

SOLDIER: My job was to go out looking for Abos. They give me an area the size of England to patrol, on my own. You had to laugh, I'd drive around putting up their signs… written in English. Planes dropped leaflets—English.
Occasionally I'd see one of 'em, minding my own business, havin' a smoke. Suddenly they'd be there! Could a run me through with a spear…
[*Half in Pitjantjatjara*] … *Pitja pitja*… I was taught a few words… Big poison *puyu* coming. But you couldn't make 'em… Just hoped the fences'd keep 'em out.

 TREVOR *enters over the top of the copper shell.*

SONG: 'I'm in the Lord's Army' (a children's hymn)

SAIRA: [*sung under*]
  I'm too young to march in the infantry,
  Ride in the cavalry,
  Shoot the artillery,
  I'm too young to fly over land and sea,
  But I'm in the Lord's Army… Yes sir!
  I'm in the Lord's Army,

I'm in the Lord's Army,
I'm too young to fly over land and sea,
But I'm in the Lord's Army.

TREVOR *climbs up and stands high on the shell.*

TREVOR: Soldiers rolled out fencing, hundreds of miles, across our country. My family, walking, from waterhole to waterhole. Know how far they can travel. They come to a fence. It's too far to turn back, can't climb over, die like vermin at a rabbit proof fence, *maliki ya nyinangu ngura tjanampangka.* [pests in their own country.] *Ilungu.* [Finished.]

TREVOR *walks down the shell to* JULIE.

YUMI *rolls across floor along the white path towards* TREVOR.

TREVOR *picks up* JULIE *and carries her past the* CHOIR, *as if she has passed away.*

The CHOIR *stand and sing the Creedence Clearwater Revival song 'Bad Moon Rising' in Pitjantjatjara language.*

SCREEN: *The moon passes.*

YUMI *dances as* TREVOR *moves back to centre stage.*

SCENE EIGHT

TREVOR, *as* YOUNG ARNOLD, *is curled up in the mission asleep and crying. He looks up out of a window. He comments on what he sees.*

TREVOR: And so my father, little Arnold, a boy… is there… in Cundalee Refugee Camp… in the mission dorm, *tjitji kutjupa tjutangka.* [with the other children.] But his mother likes to be outside by the fire, under the stars. He wants his *ngunytju*, she's out there somewhere. Wants his father, but Tjamu Jack is not back yet *walytja tjutaku ngurinyi.* [from finding more family.]

The sound of a truck arriving.

TREVOR, *as* YOUNG ARNOLD, *is peeking out the window.*

TREVOR *also becomes the* MOTHER *and* FATHER *in the scene.*

That night he hears it… *Walytja piruku,* [More family, more *walytja,*] in Tjamu Jack's truck. There's Tjamu Jack helping them down. Arnold can't see his *ngunytju*, she should be there to meet him now. Tjamu Jack is looking too… Ahhh, here she comes… *Ka paluṟu palya wiya, tjina kali-kali pitjani, patalatjara…* [but she's not right, walking funny, got a bottle…] other men. Tjamu Jack is angry now, hits her, pulls a spear on her, she's on the ground. Arnold drops back on the bed, his *ngunytju* is finished. Next morning *Paluṟu anu…* [Tjamu Jack is gone…] Not with Mr Stewart, with the bully-men. Arnold doesn't know where.

> YOUNG ARNOLD *flops back down on the bed and then rolls away upstage.*
>
> *A second bomb.*

SCENE NINE

The sound of crows.

SCREEN: *The shadow of* MRS BLAIR.

LEX *tells the* SOLDIER*'s story in shadow, behind the screen.*

TREVOR *momentarily becomes a crow (as in Scene One).*

SOLDIER: Testing one bomb at Maṟalinga, there was a wind shift, and a radioactive cloud passed over Adelaide.

> TREVOR, *as the crow, calls.*

TREVOR: In Adelaide, Hazel Blair watches her son Tony playing. Above them, a crow calls and flies off into a strange red cloud. Mrs Blair sends Tony inside… and takes the washing from the line.

SOLDIER: A scientist—Hedley Marsden—thinking the 'Weapons Test Safety Committee' were puppets, ran his own tests on farm animals… for radioactive iodine 'n' strontium-90. Strontium-90 gets in the food chain, into school milk, causes bone cancer.

> JULIE *slowly enters as a figure.*
>
> *A third bomb.*
>
> TREVOR *makes his way to the pile of bones.*
>
> JULIE *walks across the stage.*

TREVOR: *Aṉangu tjina ananyi munu tjitji kulunypa tjuṯa katinyi…* [*Walytja*, carrying little ones…] *nintiya kutjupa kutjupa kuṟa ngaranyi, utuwaṟi nyanganyi...* [they know something is wrong, see the clouds...] *tjitji paku pu<u>t</u>u tjina ananyi...* [children too tired to walk...] *Tjamu kami pikatjara, ngururpa wantikatingu,* [Elders too sick, left by the road,] to wait for trucks that never come. *Walytja tju<u>t</u>a kulpingka kumpini...* [Families hiding in caves...] till the sticky cloud passes... refugees.

TREVOR *pushes down the pile of bones and starts making a circle out of them as he talks.*

A fourth bomb.

SOLDIER: Why did ASIO think Marston a 'scientist of counterespionage interest'? Why did they make him delete his results? Why did pathologists secretly steal 21,830 bones from dead children during autopsy, to test for strontium-90?

SONG: *'Urungka Tjarpara-Tjarpara'* ('The Swimming Song')

The introductory beat of 'Urungka Tjarpara-Tjarpara' *('The Swimming Song') plays under the following:*

TREVOR: When my family came out of the caves *miri tju<u>t</u>a tjara-tjaranu miinga pu<u>r</u>unpa.* [bodies were scattered like black ants.] *Tjamu kutju tjina anu, tjananya kurultjunkula ka palu<u>r</u>u pikatjararingu ku<u>l</u>u... ilungu.* [One *tjamu* walked back in burying them, he too got sick... finished.]

JULIE *enters, making a circle of white dust around the copper shell.*

The SOLDIER *comes from behind the screen and enters, upstage of the shell.*

SOLDIER: Why were British soldiers given protective clothing while we wandered in army shorts and no shirt... guinea pigs, tested for radiation? How come our families get so sick...?

A fifth bomb.

TREVOR: [*Nyanganka kutjuparinyi...* [Something is happening here...] Strange dusty, *ulpu<u>r</u>ul-ulpu<u>r</u>u,* [sticky cloud,]
Feel it, touch their... *kata...*

The CAST *repeat* 'kata'.

Feel it, touch their... *a<u>l</u>ipi<u>r</u>i...*

The CAST *repeat* 'a<u>l</u>ipi<u>r</u>i'.

Feel it, touch their... *mu<u>t</u>i...*

The CAST *repeat* 'mu*t*i'.

Feel it, touch their… *tjina.*

The CAST *repeat* 'tjina'.

SONG: *'Kata, Alipiri, Muti, Tjina'* ('Heads and Shoulders, Knees and Toes') reprise

CHOIR: [*sung slowly and mournfully*]
*Kata, alipiri, muti, tjina,
Muti tjina, muti tjina,
Kata alipiri, muti, tjina,
Pina, kuru, winpinpi, mulya.*

The singing continues under the following:

SOLDIER: They promised it was safe, but one morning, after a test, we find a bunch of Aboriginals camped, in the middle of the crater?! Threw the poor buggers in the Jeep, frightened and moaning. Hosed 'em, 'n' scrubbed 'em, till their skin was raw and bleeding. No female personnel, so we had to do it. Pregnant one lost her baby. All hell broke lose—special agents, secrecy agreements. Eventually, put 'em in a truck and drove them four hundred and forty miles away, just like that.

A seventh bomb.

YUMI *enters, raking, making a sun pattern in the white dust on the black sand, before moving off.*

TREVOR: *Ngayuku walytja tjara-tjaranu,* [So my people are split up,] refugees now, taken east and south, and Arnold, west to Cundalee, bundled on freight trains… *Tjana ngurpa.* [They don't know where.]

A tenth bomb.

SOLDIER: Why'd we keep bombing them? Each one a thousand times Hiroshima. City folk thought it was a few bombs, to help save us from the commies. How many tests? A dozen, was it? And the six hundred smaller tests, the twenty-two kilos of plutonium, the twelve years we bombed 'em, twice as long as World War Two… But do you see them in the RSL or marching on ANZAC Day?

The SOLDIER *moves upstage around the shell, wiping away the pattern into the black sand.*

TREVOR: *Nganampa walytja ilunyangka,* [When our people pass on,] out of respect *nganana ini wangkantja wiya.* [we don't use their name or talk about them.] So when we were asked if people died out there, *nganana panya palunyatjara wangkantja wiya.* [we didn't talk about it.] Made it easy for government to pretend.

    YUMI *enters, climbing over the top of the shell.*

SOLDIER: Any road, I've made my peace, took a package tour to the Hiroshima gardens. Nice Japanese lady smiles at me, a *hibakusha*— person who survived the bomb... It hit me then... I've had so many mates die to this, but... they don't have a special name for us back in Oz.

TREVOR: *Kutjuparinyi,* [Changing,] *uwankara kutjuparingu.* [everything changed now.] Split up... but not finished... refugees.

    AMANYI, *an elder, stops the show and speaks slowly to the audience. She tells a story in Pitjantjatjara of her experience of the bomb as a child. It is translated by* PANTJITI. *As* AMANYI *finishes:*

PANTJITI: Trevor, finish that story.

TREVOR: And remember Tony Blair's mother? Died of a rare cancer, her little boy grew up to be in charge of that British nation, who bombed us in their cold war.

    A final bomb—the sound far away.

    The CHOIR *sing* 'Tjituru Tjituru' *(a Pitjantjatjara language version of the David Bowie song 'Sorrow').*

    During the song the house lights go up a little.

    The young people in the CAST *carry small ceramic bowls of pure white powder they have been grinding up through the performance. Walking into the auditorium, while the song is sung, they pour a little into the hands of people in the audience.*

    The CAST *walk around the copper shell as they sing* 'Tjituru Tjituru' *and continue singing as they exit offstage with the* YOUNG PEOPLE *following.*

    TREVOR *is alone. He picks up a 'Winnie the Pooh' book and enters from behind the shell, kneeling downstage centre.*

SCENE TEN

TREVOR *reads an excerpt from 'Winnie the Pooh' by A.A. Milne in which the characters Kanga, Baby Roo, Rabbit and Pooh appear. He reads in character voices as if reading to a group of children.*

TREVOR: [*gently*] A.A. Milne couldn't have known that Kangaroo—*Malu*—is sacred to us. It's like stealing the baby Jesus. I wonder why people don't know that?
I wonder why it is that when people visit the Eiffel Tower they know how to say 'hello' in French?
And I wonder why people who come to Pitjantjatjara country, to visit Ularu, don't khow to say 'hello' in Pitjantjatjara?
I wonder,
I wonder if people know we're refugees?
I wonder who has heard our beautiful land rights song?
No wonder people always say, 'Aha…' when they hear stories about us.

A film starts. The CAST *enter one at a time, slowly, during the film. They stand, scattered across the stage, watching the film.*

SCENE ELEVEN

SCREEN: *In this film scene* JANGALA's *daughter,* KIRA, *is with* JANGALA *at a party. She has big red boxing gloves on. It's dark.*

JANGALA: *[to the camera] Say, 'Hello… my name's Shakira. I'm three.'*
KIRA: *Jangala Jamieson. I'm three.*
JANGALA: *Say, 'My name's Shikira Jane Jamieson'.*

She repeats the name, punching with the boxing gloves.

Cut to: her talking on a toy phone.

FELLA: *Who is it?*
KIRA: *Peter.*
FELLA: *Peter who?*
KIRA: *Peter Pumpkin.*

Cut to:

FELLA: *Any kangaroo tail?*

JANGALA: *Ring pet shop for Daddy for kangaroo tails. Say Daddy wants six tails.*
KIRA: *Six tails.*

Cut to:

JANGALA: *Ring up, talk to Mum, come pick you up now.*
KIRA: *No.*
JANGALA: *Mum come pick you up?*
KIRA: *No, Daddy.*
JANGALA: *Take you home?*
KIRA: *I'll set the police on you.*

FELLAS *laugh.*

FELLA: *[laughing] Police on you!*
JANGALA: *But why?*
KIRA: *Daddy going to jail. Take Daddy there.*
JANGALA: *But why? Daddy don't want to go to jail. Daddy want to stay with Kira.*
KIRA: *[picking up the phone] Yes, don't. Don't come, don't take Daddy.*
JANGALA: *Oh, don't take Daddy. Tell the policeman.*
KIRA: *They gone.*
JANGALA: *Tell 'em go home.*
KIRA: *You go home. You go home, policeman.*
JANGALA: *Leave Daddy alone.*
KIRA: *Leave Daddy alone!*

As the film ends the CHOIR *stand.*

SONG: *'Kulilaya'* ('The Land Rights Song')
CHOIR: [*sung*]
> *Kulilaya, kulilaya*
> *Ngura nganampa manta wiru*
> *Nganampa tjamuku, kamiku ngura iriti nguru*
> *Kulilaya*
> *Manta miilmiilpatjara.*
> *Tjukurpa alatjitu.*
> *Nyaaku nyura kulintja wiya?*

The CHOIR *and* CAST *move back to their positions, leaving* TREVOR *alone, centre stage.*

SCENE TWELVE

The young people in the CAST *pour a circle of white powder on the black sand.*

TREVOR *'creates' the figure of* LITTLE ARNOLD, *lying on the floor in the circle.*

TREVOR *then backs away from the circle.*

TREVOR: So there was little Arnold, my dad…
With his *ngunytju* murdered,
His father in prison,
His family bombed, everyone refugees, scattered… he's alone.
His elders, watching, know life will be hard for him.
The first of a new breed, living in two worlds, a nowhere kid.
So they give him a new name, a special name, *Tjiwa*.
And, they watch as he is taken from Cundalee Refugee Camp,
To a new mission, Norseman Mission… to be growed up.
At Norseman, Arnold is shy.
He's from the bush, little bit of English,
He's lonely,
He doesn't like the roof over his head,
He wants the stars,
He doesn't like the cold,
He wants the campfire glow,
The warmth of camp dogs,
He wants his family,
But, at Norseman, they lock you up if you cry,
They chain you to the clothesline and flog you if you run away, so…
Arnold runs away.
They bring him back.
They lock him up,
He runs away,
They bring him back,
They flog him.
All the while he's growing, growing,
Now he steals a car to run away,
Should he run to his *ngura*?

Music from a Pitjantjatjara language version of the Burt Bacharach and Hal David song 'This Guy's in Love with You' begins under as the CHOIR *stand.*

Where the poison *manta* will get on his skin and kill him?
Tjiwa, my father, is a nowhere kid, without his country, what is he?
Without his country, who is he?

The CHOIR *begins the song.*

The day he saw her,
A little *kungawara*,
He was thirteen, she was thirteen…

He joins the CHOIR *in singing the song.*

During the instrumental break, TREVOR *is handed a microphone and has his jacket put on, becoming a corny cabaret idol.*

He finishes with the song.

Arnold liked her, Gail.
He found out why she looked after the little ones,
She knew what it was like for them,
She'd been left with the missionaries, when she was eighteen days old.
Her *ngunytju* [mother] left her thrupence, in her sock,
So she could buy lollies when she grew up…
Always said her *ngunytju* would be coming back,
And then she'd buy lollies, and share with her mother,
But her *ngunytju* never came back…
Now Gail had Arnold… and Arnold had Gail.
He stopped running away then.

The CHOIR *sing the chorus of the song, as slabs of clay are brought out.* ELTON *and* TREVOR *watch on as the clay is brought to them.*

When they are old enough, and they've left the mission they decide to *altinyi*, marry. But should they *altinyi*? Would this be a wrong-way marriage? Who do they ask?

The three men in the CAST *begin pounding the clay slabs on the floor.*

Arnold's father is in jail, so he can't come to the wedding…

But Gail's *ngunytju*…
Gail has found her now,
Told her about Arnold, asked her to the wedding,
Told her there'd be bags of mixed lollies on every table.
Big party after,
So Gail's *ngunytju*, she can come,
See her little girl, her *untalpa, altinyi*, get married,
Make something of her life after all the *tjituṟu.* [sorrow.]
And Arnold and Gail are getting ready…
Family turning up,
They are happy for Tjiwa,
He's a good boy,
Gail is happy her *ngunytju* will be there,
See her man, in his new suit… new start.
And Gail's *ngunytju* is dressed in her Sunday best,
Gail's *ngunytju* is on her way, walking,
Gail's *ngunytju* hails a taxi,
Back seat,
She sits careful, to not crease her new frock,
And on the way there,
The driver takes a wrong road,
No matter,
But she's anxious, she might be late,
Now the road is a dead-end,
This driver doesn't know what he's doing.
Now the driver has to stop the car,
And now the driver does know what he's doing……
As he *palunya punganyi,* [bashes her,] in her Sunday best,
Bashes her, with a wheel brace,
Bashes her, till Gail's *ngunytju, ngayuku kami kutjupa ilungu,*
[my other grandmother is finished,] gone.

   Pause.

And at the wedding, Gail can't wait any longer,
So Gail is walking down the aisle to Arnold,
And Gail is *pukulpa,* [happy,] but Gail is *tjituṟu-tjituṟu,* [sad,]
What's keeping her mother?
She's thinking, about her mother's smile,

Wants to hear her mother laugh,
She wants a hug,
When she sees those tables, all posh with white tablecloths,
When she sees on each one, a bag of mixed lollies…

>PANTJITI *sings a reprise of part of* 'Tjitu<u>r</u>u Tjitu<u>r</u>u' *('Sorrow')*.

>PANTJITI *and* JENNIFER *bring* irmangka irmangka *(bush medicine) to* TREVOR, *to comfort him because of the sad story. They rub the bush medicine on his wrists and forearms to help heal his grief.*

>*The clay pieces are taken and placed like gravestones near the bones.*

>*During the song* TREVOR *returns upstage to sit with these senior women in the* CHOIR. *They watch the screen.*

SCENE THIRTEEN

SCREEN: *Film scene.*

ARNOLD: *Over time, he'd try to make up to us, you know, he didn't have much time to live, you know?*

TREVOR: *Knowing what it's like? How it's like? That way.*

ARNOLD: *That's when I took him to… before we moved back to Cundalee, years before we moved there… he passed away. Dad. We never got tired of it, you know. Make up for the lost time, you know, he spent in prison.*

TREVOR: *All I can remember when I was very young child, a toddler. He had the best embrace.*

ARNOLD: *Jangala is the same. That's why I spend a lot of time with him… Jangala, he's good one time and the next, he'll go off and then come good… I won't say I spent most of my time with him but I try with you and you're back down this way… and with him… So that's why I'm thinking about going up north to spend time with you.*

TREVOR: *Yeah.*

ARNOLD: *So then when I find out Jangala's okay then I will.*

SCENE FOURTEEN

After the film TREVOR *walks to the shell and has a piss, becoming a drunk* TJILIPI *begging.*

TJILPI: [*to the audience*] 'Ere! Come 'ere, p'ease, lit'a'bit'a'money… for my people, p'ease?
LEX: [*off*] Here you go, Jacky Jacky, go buy yourself a hamburger.
TJILPI: Thanks, thanks, thanks very much… [*a quiet aside*] white cun'.
TREVOR: See that old man there, old *tjilpi*. He smells real strong, very important man. See him there, pissed his pants, little bit of sick on his shirt. For us that's, like seeing Don Bradman there, pissing his pants. One of your *wati initjara*. [important men.]
Over the years, a lot of our people have drifted into town…
Arnold and Gail, are both orphaned and *altingu,* [married,] and
They want to make something of themselves,
Gail trains to be nurse,
She helps when the *yungupala putingka wirtjapakani,* [boys are running in the bush,]
When they come back dehydrated…
Arnold's a policeman,
If something goes wrong, in Kalgoorlie,
When our people come to town, party up,
The natural place to stay is a bush hotel, in the park there…
So for a while Arnold works with the police,
He bring them back to camp to dry out,
And Gail is helping with the babies.
Then they have three boys of their own, Jarrod, Jangala and me.
The next generation, *ngura walytjangka wiya nyinanyi.* [away from country.]

    TREVOR *becomes a two-year-old holding his aunty's hand.*

And when I'm two,
The *kungkas* take me from my *ngunytju,*
Go bush, put me down on wobbly legs,
Make me walk straight away,
Rub out my footprints—give me a new name…
Kanmatju,
Which means 'Swift as a Spear…'
And so us boys grow up,
Sometimes in the city,
And sometimes in our refugee camp.
But Cundalee is small,

Our nation, our *ngura*, used to be the size of Great Britain.
And the thing I notice is,
The old people are *tjituru-tjituru*, [unhappy,] they feel *tiwilpa, munu nguluntju kuliningi.* [cramped, frightened.]
Let me explain.
See, for us, when you pass away, when you're finished,
Very important time,
You have a *tjukurpa*, [totem,] maybe a *walawuru*, [eagle,] or a *malu* or a *tinka* [goanna] totem, and, after you die, your spirit enters one of your totem,
For me... one of these here.
   He indicates the eagle.
Ka nyuntu wiyaringkula, nyuntunya kurultjunanyi tjukaruru...
[But your body when it's finished, has to be buried, right way...]
There would be *inma pulka...* [big ceremony...]
   The sound of crows and music.
Miri [The body] would be *kurultjungkula,* [buried,]
Then a year later, dug up and placed on a platform in trees,
Let the sun and birds clean up the *tarka.* [bones.]
Then later, you come back, reburial.
Can't say their name for a certain time.
You must not go there, *miri ngarinyi,* [where the body is,]
Can't walk on their grave, and so,
When someone *ilungu* [died] everyone would *pakara ananyi.* [move camp.]
We're very sensitive to these real things...
And so because of the sorrow and the poison,
Many, many people are dying,
Strange *iluntja*, cancer *iluntja*, alcohol *iluntja.*
Living at Cundalee was like living in a cemetery,
The old people, *tiwilpa kulinu,* [felt hemmed in, cramped,] *nguluntju,*
Can't walk anywhere,
No room for ceremony.
Cundalee Refugee Camp was one big sorrow place.

SCREEN: *Slow motion film runs behind the scene. It shows the Cundalee camp is in a bad way.*

Old people want to go back to country,
To move around,
Manta kilinakutu. [To the clean red sand.]
Anangu rawa nyinanyi pikatjara cancer-nguru,
[But people still sick from the cancer,]
Drift into Kalgoorlie, to be near a doctor,
Live in parks...
Split up more and more, refugees...
> TREVOR *becomes* TJILIPI *again.*

TJILPI: *Puyu* p'ease... p'ease, for my people?

SCENE FIFTEEN

The CHOIR *stand. They sing part of* 'Ngayunya Wantirialku' *(a Pitjantjatjara language version of Bob Dylan's song 'I Shall Be Released').*

As the song finishes, prison doors open.

TREVOR, *as* TJAMU JACK—*an old man now—walks out stiff and sore.*

TREVOR: Eventually, Tjamu Jack has served his time, twenty years. He can't believe what he sees...
Old people, sleeping in parks,
Maniku patani, [Waiting for handouts,]
Dazed, shell shocked,
Everything gone.
Why did he bother saving people from the bombs,
Ngura walytja wantikatinyi? [Leaving the homelands... for this to happen?]
Paluru pitjangu ngananala nyinantjikitja, [He comes to stay with us,] *walytja.*

TJAMU JACK: Trebba! Cup a tea... Trebba!

YOUNG TREVOR: Ohhh, game on 'ere!

TV ANNOUNCER: And... and Cable, drop punt.... snaps a goaalllll...

YOUNG TREVOR: Mum! Tjamu Jack calling out there... Orrr, why do I have to do it, every time? 'S not fuckin' fair, I don' wanna fuckin' havta fuckin' do it all the fuckin' time, always fuckin' me who gets the cup a fuckin' tea. What 'bout fuckin' Jangala, he never has to fuckin' do it... [*Suddenly nice*] Heh, Tjamu Jack, cup of tea, okay.

TJAMU JACK: *Tjantju tjamu ngalya pitja ampuntjaku.* [Thank you, grandson, come here. Give me a hug.]

He gives TREVOR *a big hug.*

Warpuwa, warpuwa, aralta. [Hurry hurry, piss off then.]
Trebba, Trebba, did you ask your dad for me?
YOUNG TREVOR: Yes, Tjamu Jack/
TJAMU JACK: Ask again, I want to see Cundalee, one last time…
YOUNG TREVOR: Okay, Tjamu/
TREVOR: Took him back, to Cundalee.
That night we *ngura tjunu,* [camped there,] *ngamu ngaringu.* [slept real close.]
Ngura mamutjara, [Cundalee was haunted,]
Heard stones, thrown on the tin roof of the tumbledown mission,
Stayed close to Tjamu Jack… *wati rawa witulyangka.* [powerful man still.]
Through the trees, *waru tjuta kampanyi,* [campfires burning,] no-one there,
Stayed in close.
In the morning,
Tjamu Jack was gone…
Found him standing at the foot of the grave of his wife, by the gate, at Cundalee.
Kuri palumpa kurultjunkulala.
He knew he was finished, *kuwari wiyarinyi.*
Word gets around,
He's out of prison…
Her people coming, payback, *ngapartji,*
Walpangka ananyi palunya ngurintjikitja,
Travelling on the wind to find him…
He knew,
He'd never see the red *manta* of his homelands,
His *ngura* where he'd rescued the *walytja* from the cold war,
He knew then,
All the *yangupala tjuta ananyi,* [young people were drifting,]
The *tjukurpa irititjaku ngurparingu,* [old ways forgotten,]
Feeling shame speaking Pitjantjatjara… not speaking Pitjantjatjara,
Wondered why he'd bothered bringing the *walytja* out.

The CHOIR *stands.*

SONG: 'The Old Rugged Cross'

The CHOIR *sings under the following dialogue.*

TREVOR: Few months later,
Palunya kurultjunu [Buried him] on top of his wife,
My grandmother,
The woman he killed,
By the gates at Cundalee, final resting place for Tjamu Jack, our first refugee.

The CHOIR *sing* 'Parpakalkuna' *(a Pitjantjatjara language version of the hymn 'I'll Fly Away').*

TREVOR *lies down on the shell. He closes his eyes with his fingers and folds his arms over his chest.*

The young people in the CAST *carry over two small bowls and drop dust along his body, making a shape around him in white powder.*

They leave a bowl on the edge of the stage.

They walk back to their seats.

SCENE SIXTEEN

After a moment TREVOR *sits up.*

TREVOR: Not everyone was lying around in the park,
With a cask of cheap moselle as a pillow.
Some people speak up to the government with us,
Royal Commission,
Diamond Jim McClelland.
We have to go to London,
Make the English feel sorry…
[*In a bush tone*] But who should go, to speak for us about being refugees?
There's my *tjamu*—Hughie Windlass.

OLD FELLA: *Ai Hughie nyuntu nganampa ankuntjaku Londontakutu.*

HUGHIE: *Ewa*, I'll go… London, eh… who's dat London?

TREVOR: We give him presents to take,
Something special from our country,
Thirteen bags of sand for the judges.

On the plane Hughie feels confident,
Sitting back in business class.

> HUGHIE *tries the headphones—loud music. He finds the right channel. And sings a couple of lines from the Peter Allen song 'I Still Call Australia Home', with reference to London.*
>
> *He steps off the plane looking around at the size of the place.*

TREVOR: When Hughie got off that plane,
What he saw nearly destroyed our case…
Takeaway shops everywhere/
COCKNEY COOK: Whot c'n 'r git ya, gov? Pork pie? Toad in the 'ole? Beef wellington?
HUGHIE: *Hamburger uwani please.*
TREVOR: Ate so many he was late to court every day… we changed his name to Hamburger!
Last day in court,
Hughie has said nothing.
Finally it his turn,
Gives his presents to the judges…
HUGHIE: *Paki. Munta,* [Sand,] Your Honour/
JUDGE: [*posh*] Oh really, how very kind/
HUGHIE: Feel it, Your Honour… *Marangku ularpuwa. Wiṟu panya.* Rub your hands in it… Lovely, isn't it, Your Worship, sirs/
JUDGE: Lovely yes, well thank you, we'll treasure that a great deal/
HUGHIE: *Nganampa nguranguṟu,* [From our country,] Your Honour, *nyura bomb waningu.* [where you dropped those bombs there.]

> *The* JUDGE *yells, scared by the radioactive sand.*
>
> *A bomb sound.*

I frightened that little mouse under her chair.
TREVOR: Came home with thirteen million dollars… hamburgers for all of us!

> TREVOR *dances around the stage in mock joy. The* WOMEN *join in—sexy dancing.*
>
> *The are on their feet.*
>
> *The* CHOIR *sing a dance mix reprise of part of* 'Wantiriyalani' *('Once in a Lifetime').*

SCENE SEVENTEEN

TREVOR: Once we had fifty thousand years,
　Now we had thirteen million dollars,
　Once we had a country bigger than Great Britain,
　Now we had thirteen million,
　(About the price of a waterfront property in Sydney)
　The oldest language in the world,
　Now... Woolworths shares.
　We are grateful, help pay our medical bills, chemotherapy,
　Help buy the alcohol,
　Help to numb our feelings,
　On the park benches there...

He becomes OLD TJILPI *again.*

OLD TJILPI: [*sung*]
　Wantiraiyani/ kapingku_n_itju witini
　Letting the days go by/ water flowing underground...

He asks the audience for money.

Mani uwa, please? Got a wife in hospital...

He uses a begging bowl with the audience.

TREVOR: Not everybody is *tjitu_r_u*.
　These women here, senior women, important women... don't believe the cliche.
　Some of our old people were determined to go back,
　Live as close to our *ngura* as possible,
　Maybe wait there for that half-life thing... only twenty-five thousand years.
　But we can wait.

The sound of an excavator. TREVOR *is in front of the grader as an* UNCLE, *signalling which way to go. Calling out in language:*

UNCLE: *Pitja, pitja*... this way, through here.

TREVOR: So, in 1986,
　My *walytja*,
　Spend some of that money,
　Buy an excavator, make a road back out to country...

UNCLE: *Nyangawanu, nyangawanu pitjama. Pitja, pitja...* [This way, keeping going through here...]
[*Seeing a footprint*] 'Ere, something 'ere... footprints...

> *He signals the excavator to stop. The diesel slows and chugs. He tracks the footprints.*

TREVOR: *Tjina,* [Footprints,] they know those feet from thirty years ago, *Tjana tjina wananu,* [They track them,]
And they find Mr Rictor *munu palumpa walytja...* [and his family...]
Been living in *kulpi nyarangka,* [cave there,]
Big reunion,
And they bring them back to Kalgoorlie,
Where, just twenty years ago, they meet white people for the first time... 'cause of that bomb.

> *The sound of a bomb.*

> YUMI, *the Japanese dancer, enters, rolling slowly across the floor as if by a huge force in Hiroshima... or like spinifex across the Australian desert. She rolls into* TREVOR *and they both roll off.*

> JULIE *walks across the stage, following them—a reprise of the journey cut off by the fence in Scene Seven.*

> JANGALA *is seen shadow boxing hard, sweating.*

SCENE EIGHTEEN

Upstage in silhouette, JANGALA *keeps shadow boxing during the scene transition.*

TREVOR: *Tjilpi tjuṯa munu pampa tjuṯa* [Old people] have built their road go back out,
And they want us *aṉangu kuḻunypa tjuṯa tjanala ankuntjaku.* [young ones to go back with them.]
But the young people, mostly want to go to town,
Kalgoorlie...
Doing blockies in Commodores,
Play footie,
Tjikila [Drink]... Emu Export... old *Kalaya* himself,
Party up...
My brother Jangala, he sees it both ways,

He knows the bush,
But he likes it in town,
He likes to party,
Mukuringanyi, [Likes the grog,]
Kungka tjutaku mukuringanyi, [Likes his womans,]
Mukuringanyi [Likes] his fists when he drinks…
He drinks with his woman.
And he is like our Tjamu Jack…
I love my brother Jangala…
I haven't finished my film yet…
I think it's about *walytja*.

   The CAST *and* CHOIR *stand watching the following film.*

SCREEN: *The film shows an argument between* JANGALA *and* MUM *and* TREVOR. JANGALA *is about to explode. He cries. His kids sit on the bonnet of his car.*

TREVOR: *No, I mean fuck you.*

MUM: *No you.*

TREVOR: *It's fuckin' bullshit, he nearly got picked up. Look, I'm fuckin' serious.*

   JANGALA *sits down holding his head.*

I mean it! Mum, tell him please.

MUM: *[to* JANGALA*] That's making your head no good. You want to get a good life.*

   She is holding his face and wiping his eyes.

TREVOR: *[to* JANGALA*] I love you. I'll get you a good fuckin' place where you can sit around.*

   JANGALA *crys.*

JANGALA: *I'm getting out of here. I'm getting out of here soon.*

MUM: *You go with Trevor to Broome.*

JANGALA: *This town is mucking me about here. But no life here really, I was just born and bred here. I've got to show everybody who I am. Take it from me, I don't go looking for trouble, it comes to me. It's… I'm too good for all the little dogs around here. That's why they get me pissed. [Crying] It's not my fault, man.*

MUM: *You're right.*

JANGALA: Too much pressure.
MUM: Look at that over there, you've got two beautiful little kids.
JANGALA: Uwa.
MUM: They want a daddy.
JANGALA: Uwa.
MUM: They want to get hooked up to somebody. That's why I brought them up here so you can have 'em.
JANGALA: But the alcohol's fuckin' me up. I love you, Mum…
MUM: Alright.
TREVOR: Palya.

>TREVOR *and* MUM *both hug him.*
>
>WALYTJA *(*FAMILY*) enter and stand facing the screen watching the film. In the darkness* JANGALA *enters the stage area unnoticed and sits on the black sand amongst their feet.*
>
>*The film ends.*
>
>*On stage, four small bowls of powder are put around* JANGALA.
>
>*The* CHOIR *move back to their seats, leaving* JANGALA *centre stage.*

SCENE NINETEEN

TREVOR *climbs down over the copper shell.*

He places a piece of clay in the middle of the shell.

The CAST *carry baskets full of pieces of broken clay* ngura *(country). They place them around the shell, and then go and bring people from the audience. They sit with them, passing the pieces of clay to them. Together they lay them out on the shell as though putting something back together.*

TREVOR *stands in the middle of the shell.*

TREVOR: Before birth,
  Your *kurunpa* [spirit] shimmers across the *manta,* [land,] searching,
  Looking for your tiny unborn body to rest in—*tjarrinpa.*
  Tjarrinpa creates your own *tjukurpa,*
  Your *tjukurpa* gives you responsibilities for your *ngura.*

  >*The* CAST *begin putting the broken pieces back together.*

  And so, you are born…

And where *ngunytjulu nyuntunya mantangka tjunu,* [mother first lets you touch the earth,]
This is a *ngura miilmiilpa,* [special place,] you have special responsibilities to look after it.
A *tjukula* [waterhole] maybe, a *tali* [sand dune] or a *puli*... [rock...]
Your *ngunytju* is a *minyma kunpu.* [strong women.]
And while you are still tiny,
She may *tjina parari mulapa ankula* [walk a long way] from where you first touched the *manta.*
And these places are your *atunymankuntjaku* [responsibility] too,
Ngura ngururpa tjuta kulu... [All the land between...]
And *tjukurpa,*
Won't let you forget your *atunymankuntjaku* [duties] from your birth, and...
Tjukurpa,
Is real,
If you can't fulfill your *atunymankuntjaku...* [responsibilities...]
you'll *tjituru-tjitururiku* [fret] deep within,
If you can't be where you belong... you'll *nyurkarinkuku,* [whither,]
And if you can't look after your *ngura*... it will *kurunpa kurarinkuku...* [suffer...]
You also have your *walytja*... big family!
You have the places your dad was responsible for—your mama's *ngura*—*ngura panya palumpa ngura walytja* [the country to which he belongs.]
More *atunymananyi...* [responsibilities]...
And your *ngunytju* and her *ngura,*
You have to look after these too...
And then there's your *malanypa* [brothers] and *kangkuru...* [sisters...]
You have to look after *tjanampa ngura...* [their places...]
And then... you get *altiku...* [married...] *piruku* [more] to look after!
[*To confuse*] Maybe your birthplace is in the same place as your cousin's birthplace, but your father's is in the same place as your aunty's cousin's mama's... and you fellas wonder why we never and get a job... we're too busy, eh.
Funny, isn't it... for tonight I just wanted to make a film about my *malanypa.* [brother.]

Throughout the following film, JANGALA *pours 'poisonous' white powder—that has been ground up during the performance—on his arms in a line from each bowl.*

TREVOR *steps off the copper shell and watches this last film.*

SCENE TWENTY

SCREEN: *This film shows trees burning in the background.* TREVOR *and* JANGALA *and* FRIENDS *are drinking around a big fire, listening to music from a car stereo. They are telling stories.*

JANGALA: Good luck! Luck come my way. From inside.
When you go hunting and you eat malu, you always cook it half cooked and half raw. That way you always got your kapi, from the blood, the water, from the blood when you're travelling and you got the feed, the kuga. Traditional way, we used to that way. That one malu. Us ananngu. But you always cook it half cooked, half raw. Because when you travel you can sip the blood for water. Same time when you hungry, you eat the meat. That's ananngu way. Wangkata way. The traditional way. From years ago. Before we got introduced to KFC, McDonald's, Hungry Jack's and even this. [He holds up a can of beer.] That's what makes us even more silly, Any wonder we always finding ourselves in bloody trouble all the bloody time.

TREVOR: Don't drink.

JANGALA: Well, we got introduced to it... so I dunno.
I love you, my family.

TREVOR: I'm not a nigger, I'm an 'Aboriginal'.

JANGALA: My family, my coons, so they called us years ago. I love you coons…
I love you mixed breeds. Yeah, mixed breeds.

Fire, dancing from the group, the car stereo.

On stage, JANGALA *continues pouring the sand from the small bowls onto himself.*

SCENE TWENTY-ONE

A guitar is brought to TREVOR.

During the following song the CAST *take the audience members back to their seats and give each of them a little clay bowl that the* YOUNG PEOPLE *have been making during the show.*

TREVOR *sings the first part of* 'Ngayunya Wantirialku' *('I Shall Be Released').*

TREVOR: Because of the radiation, a lot of our *walytja* have gone now… but lucky for us, we're good little breeders… we got lots of teenage mums, popping them out, eh!
Won't be long, for you whitefellas, with your low birthrate, there'll only be a few of you left, living in camps on the edge of the city… But it's okay, when we pass you in the street, we'll give you a few dollars… ease your dying pillow, eh… *ngapartji ngapartji.*

> *He gives the 'important man' with the bad smell in the front row some spare change.*
>
> *He introduces us to* JANGALA.

This is my brother—Jangala.

> JANGALA *stands and looks at everyone in the audience as* TREVOR *continues with the song.*
>
> JANGALA *joins* TREVOR *and they finish the song together.*

THE END

www.currency.com.au

Visit Currency Press' website now to:

- Buy your books online
- Browse through our full list of titles, from plays to screenplays, books on theatre, film and music, and more
- Choose a play for your school or amateur performance group by cast size and gender
- Obtain information about performance rights
- Find out about theatre productions and other performing arts news across Australia
- For students, read our study guides
- For teachers, access syllabus and other relevant information
- Sign up for our email newsletter

the performing arts publisher

www.ingramcontent.com/pod-product-compliance
Lightning Source LLC
Chambersburg PA
CBHW042130160426
43198CB00022B/2969